DOING YOUR OWN TAXE

(Tax Year 2018)

Milton G. Boothe, EA

"Doing Your Taxes is as Easy as 1, 2, 3" by Milton G. Boothe, EA

The Changes Under the New Tax Cuts and Jobs Act of 2017

In 2017 Congress passed major tax reform legislation, known as the Tax Cuts and Jobs Act of 2017 (TCJA). Theses changes relating to the Act's provisions will affect the tax returns of almost every single taxpayer. These changes, however, are temporary in nature and generally apply beginning in 2018 and ending on December 31, 2025. Accordingly, most of the provisions of the Act applicable to individual taxpayers will expire in 2026. Below is a brief overview of the changes.

New Individual and Capital Gains Tax Rates

The Act maintains the current seven individual tax brackets but generally reduces the applicable tax rates. The new individual tax rates for 2018 are as follows:

1. For married taxpayers filing joint tax returns, or for surviving spouses using the Qualifying Widow(er) filing status, the rate ranges from 10% on income up to $19,050, to 37% for income of $600,000 and above.

2. For taxpayers filing Head of Household, the rate ranges from 10% on income up to $13,600, to 37% for income of $500,000 and above.

3. For single taxpayers, the rate ranges from 10% on income up to $9,525, to 37% for income of $500,000 and above.

4. For married taxpayers using the Married filing Separately filing statue, the rate ranges from 10% on income up to $9,525, to 37% for income of $300,000 and above.

For capital gains taxes, the new tax act generally continues the maximum tax rate imposed on net capital gain and qualified dividends. Accordingly, net long-term capital gain and qualified dividends are generally taxed at 0%, 15% or 20% depending on taxable income and filing status as shown in below:

1. Married Filing Jointly and Qualifying Widow(er): 0% for taxpayers earning taxable income up to $77,200; 15% for taxable income between $77,200 and $479,000; 20% for taxable income over $479,000.

2. Head of Household: 0% for taxpayers earning taxable income up to $51,700; 15% for taxable income between $51,700 and $452,400; 20% for taxable income over $452,400.

3. Single: 0% for taxpayers earning taxable income up to $38,600; 15% for taxable income between $38,600 and $425,800; 20% for taxable income over $425,800.

4. Married Filing Separately: 0% for taxpayers earning taxable income up to $38,600; 15% for taxable income between $38,600 and $239,500; 20% for taxable income over $239,500.

The New Standard Deduction Rates

One very important change under the new act is the substantially increased Standard Deduction for 2018. Under the new law, standard deductions have been increased to the following amounts:

- $24,000 for married couples whose filing status is Married Filing Jointly and surviving spouses who use the Qualifying Widow(er) filing status.

- $12,000 for taxpayers filing Single and married couples whose choose to use the Married Filing Separately filing status.

- $18,000 for taxpayers using the Head of Household filing status.

A taxpayer who can be claimed as a dependent is generally limited to a smaller standard deduction, regardless of whether the individual is actually claimed as a dependent. For 2018 returns, the standard deduction for a dependent is the greater of:
- $1,050; or
- The dependent's earned income from work for the year plus $350 (but not more than the standard deduction amount attributable to that taxpayer).

Elderly and/or blind taxpayers receive an additional standard deduction amount added to the basic standard deduction. The additional standard deduction for a blind taxpayer (a taxpayer whose vision is less than 20/200) and for a taxpayer who is age 65 or older at the end of the year is:
- $1,300 for married individuals; and
- $1,600 for singles and heads of household.
These amounts would be doubled if a taxpayer is both blind and over 65.

Personal Exemptions

Another significant change under the act is the reduction to zero of the personal exemption. In other words, beginning in tax year 2018, taxpayers can NO longer claim their dependents on their tax returns.

Child Tax Credit

Under the new act, the child tax credit has been increased from $1,000 to $2,000 for each qualifying child on a taxpayer's tax return, who has a valid social security number. Note, however, that the credit may be reduced if: (a) the taxpayer's modified adjusted gross income is more than $400,000 if married filing jointly, or (b), $200,000 if using any filing status other than married filing jointly.

In addition to increasing the amount of the child tax credit that may be applied, the new act also expanded the credit. Under this credit expansion, a taxpayer may be eligible for a partial Child Tax Credit of up to $500 with respect to:

- A dependent other than a child. That could be a dependent parent or sibling, or
- A qualifying child for whom a credit is disallowed solely because the taxpayer failed to include the child's Social Security number on the tax return for the taxable year.

Adjustments to Income

The following expenses, which were formerly deductible as adjustments to income are no longer deductible under the new act:

1. Moving Expenses (except for military relocations). Consequently, any reimbursement received from an employer for such expenses must now be included in the employee's taxable income.
2. Alimony – Under the new act, alimony payments can no longer be deducted on the payer's income tax return; neither is the recipient any longer required to report such amounts as income.

Itemized Deductions (Schedule A) Changes

Medical expenses - The new act reduced the applicable threshold for the deduction of unreimbursed medical and dental expenses to 7.5% of adjusted gross income (AGI) for the years 2017 and 2018. Formerly, only medical expenses that exceeded 10% of AGI were deductible. However, beginning in 2019, the rule reverts back to the original threshold; only medical and dental expenses that exceed 10% of AGI will be deductible - for all taxpayers regardless of age.

State and local taxes - Taxes paid by an itemizing taxpayer have generally been a deductible item on the taxpayer's federal income tax return without limit. Beginning in 2018, the new act now limits the Schedule A tax deduction for state and local taxes to $10,000 ($5,000 for married taxpayers filing separately)

Mortgage interest - The new act made the following changes to the existing home mortgage interest deduction for taxable years 2018 through 2025:

- Interest paid on home equity loans and lines of credit incurred after December 15, 2017 is not tax-deductible unless the proceeds were used to buy, build or substantially improve the taxpayer's home that secures the loan.

- Taxpayers can deduct Interest paid on home mortgages incurred after December 15, 2017, only on the amount on mortgages up to $750,000 ($375,000 or less if married filing separately). Taxpayers could formerly deduct interest paid on home acquisition indebtedness of up to $1,000,000 ($500,000 or less if married filing separately).

Miscellaneous deductions – Taxpayers could formerly deduct miscellaneous expenses such as unreimbursed employee expenses and tax preparation fees, to the extent that these expenses exceed 2% of AGI. Under the new tax act, these miscellaneous itemized deductions are suspended for expenses incurred after December 31, 2017 through 2025, and consequently cannot be deducted any more.

Casualty losses
The tax treatment of personal casualty losses and thefts has been changed under the new act. These losses were formerly deductible up to a certain extent, but under the new act the itemized deduction for personal casualty and theft losses is now limited solely to losses attributable to federally-declared disasters.

Itemized deductions limitation
The new act has suspended the overall limitation that formerly existed on itemized deductions. For tax years beginning after December 31, 2017 through December 31, 2025, itemized deductions are no longer reduced for higher-income taxpayers.

Individual Mandate Penalty
Under the Affordable Care Act, taxpayers who were not covered by adequate health insurance during the year would generally be subject to a penalty. For the years after 2018, however, the new act has reduced the penalties for failing to maintain individual healthcare to zero percent. In other words, the legislation has effectively eliminated the individual mandate penalty beginning in 2019.

Kiddie Tax Rules
For 2018 through 2025, the TCJA revises the kiddie tax rules to tax a portion of a child's net unearned income at the rates paid by trusts and estates. These rates can be as high as 37% for ordinary income or, for long-term capital gains and qualified dividends, as high as 20%

Why You Should Do Your Own Taxes

When you leave your tax preparer's office each year, there are two very important questions you should be asking yourself.

Question #1: ***How secure is your personal information after you leave it with your tax preparer?***

Probably not very secure! Do they leave your paperwork lying about the place, accessible to all, after they have completed your taxes? Are their computers adequately protected by firewalls and effective anti-virus software? Is there adequate background checks done on their employees, who obviously will have unlimited access to your sensitive personal information? The honest truth is that you really don't know.

Also, you should be concerned about hackers. These criminals have been successful in hacking into supposedly very secure government computer systems; the Office of Personnel Management, and even the IRS itself come to mind immediately. These people know that they will have access to a treasure trove of personal information if they were to hack into the computers of H&R Block, Liberty Tax, or any CPA or other tax preparation office. So what is to stop them from hacking into your tax preparer's computer, which obviously will be a lot less protected than the government's computers?

By doing your taxes yourself, you could be taking a really big step in protecting your sensitive personal information, and keeping it out of the hands of criminals

Question #2: ***Are you receiving all the tax credits and deductions that you are legally entitled to?***

Chances are, you aren't! Not taking advantage of all your tax benefits, could literally translate to thousands of dollars being left on the table.

The reality is that tax professionals are usually very busy at this time of the year, trying to get as much returns done as they possibly can, ensuring that they maximize their incomes. Consequently, the time they allocate for researching specific situations will be very limited, and because everyone's personal circumstances differ, then chances are, you might not be receiving all possible tax benefits available to you, based on your particular circumstances. Doing your own taxes, however, blesses you with the luxury of time, wherein you can do your own research, including making your own calls to the IRS, to determine what tax benefits might be applicable to you. This can literally translate into thousands of dollars in your pocket.

Learning to do your own taxes is not as daunting a task as your tax professional might want you to perceive it to be. Actually, tax preparation software has come a long way in the past few years, making it so easy for you to prepare your own taxes, that it's virtually impossible not to be able to understand the process, even with absolutely no knowledge of tax laws. There is an entire myriad of relatively inexpensive tax preparation software available today, which makes this all possible, and each will allow you to prepare and e-file multiple tax returns.

At first glance you might perceive your tax return to be a very complex government form, which can only be completed by trained tax professionals. This is a great misconception, although your tax professional might want you to think this way. That could be true only to a small extent, because in actual fact, if you were to take some time to peruse this form in detail, you might probably discover that more than 75% or more of what's on the form might be totally irrelevant to your circumstances. Consequently, you could be pleasantly surprised to discover just how easy it could be to do your own taxes.

1 Understanding Your New Tax Return

In 2017 Congress passed the first major tax reform legislation in 30 years, known as the Tax Cuts and Jobs Act of 2017 (TCJA). The changes are supposed to be temporary in nature; beginning in tax year 2018 and ending on December 31, 2025. It is generally believed that this new act should simplify the tax preparation process to a certain extent. Consequently, preparing your own taxes should not as daunting a task as many of you might perceive it to be. So if your tax returns are not overly complex, you should probably give it a shot and prepare your own taxes.

Most individuals earning income in the U.S. must file a tax return. This is the law. Individuals must file a tax return using Form 1040, *U.S. Individual Income Tax Return*. This form has been significantly modified under the new act.

The New 1040 Tax Return

For many taxpayers, the new Form, 1040 will indeed make filing taxes simpler. However, for those with somewhat more complicated tax situations, this may not be the case. In addition to the familiar schedules many taxpayers have to use, such as Schedule A for itemized deductions and Schedule C for self-employment income, there are *at least six* brand-new schedules some taxpayers may need to use. These new schedules are designated by numbers instead of letters.

We will now proceed to review the new Form 1040. This form is comprised of 2 pages, and we shall proceed to review each page in detail, to provide an overview of the structure of the new U.S. individual tax return. Note that the new Form 1040 now has only 23 lines, but some taxpayers will have to complete the new Schedule 1, which has 37 lines.

Page 1

Page 1 comprises following information:

Filing Status

You must identify your filing status from the five options contained in this section, by checking the appropriate box. You can check only one box. Your filing status determines a number of things, such as:

- Whether you must file a return.
- Your standard deduction.
- Your tax rate.
- Your eligibility for certain deductions and credits.

Name, address, and Social Security number

You enter your name, address, and Social Security number in this section. If you are married you must enter the Social Security number of your spouse also, even if you are not filing a joint return.

Dependents

You must enter each dependent's name, Social Security number, and their relationship to you.

Taxpayer's signature

You are required to sign your return, and state your occupation. If you are married and are filing a joint return, your spouse must also sign the return in the designated area.

Paid preparer's signature

Your paid preparer will sign in the section designated to him or her.

<u>Third party designee</u>
You can allow the IRS to discuss your return with any person you choose, by checking the box as appropriate.

Page 2

Page 2 comprises the following information:

<u>Lines 1 - 5a.</u>
This represents the income section of your tax return. Most income that you receive is taxable. You report your income from Employment, interest, dividends, IRAs, pensions, annuities and social security on lines 1 through 5a in this section of the form. Income from other sources, such as capital gains, unemployment compensation, self-employment, rental income and farm income must be figured first on their respective schedules (D, C, E, or F) and then reported on the new Schedule 1. The total income reported on Schedule 1 (see below) is then transferred to line 6 of the new 1040 to compute total income. Note that those old lettered schedules are still around; they haven't changed. You have to complete them, too, just as you always did—in addition to Schedule 1.

<u>Line 7</u>

This represents your Adjusted Gross income. If you have adjustments to income, these will also be entered on Schedule 1, and the total subtracted from your total income on Form 1040.

Line 8
You will deduct either your standard deduction or your Schedule A itemized deductions on line 8.

Line 9
The Tax Cuts and Jobs Act has added a new tax deduction for business owners. If you receive income from a trade or business, you can benefit from the qualified business income deduction (QBI). This deduction is claimed on line 9, and represents a 20% deduction of net income received from a trade or business.

Line 10
This represents your taxable income. The amounts on line 8 and line 9 (if applicable) is subtracted from adjusted gross income (line 7) to give you taxable income on line 10.

Line 11
Tax on income represented on line 10 is computed and entered on line 11a. Any additional tax computed on Schedule 2 (see below) is entered on line 11b, and added to the tax computed on 11a, to give total tax.

Line 12.
The child tax credit/credit for other dependents is entered on line 12a. All other nonrefundable credits such as the foreign tax credit, the credit for child and dependent childcare, the education credit, and the residential energy credit are computed on Schedule 3 (see below) and entered on line 12b. The total of lines 12a and 12b is subtracted from the tax computed on line 11.

Line 13
Subtract line 12 from line 11.

Line 14
Other taxes such as household employment taxes, the health care individual responsibility payment (to go away in 2019), the net investment income tax, and the additional Medicare tax are computed on Schedule 4 (see below) and entered on line 14.

Line 15
Other taxes are added to the total on line 13 to compute total tax on line 15.

Line 16

Enter income tax withheld from W-2s and 1099s.

Line 17.
Enter all refundable credits on line 17, such as earned income credit (17a), additional child tax credit (17b), and refundable educational credits (17c). Add to these amounts any other amounts entered on Schedule 5 (see below). Schedule 5 comprises of *other payments and refundable credits*, such as estimated tax payments, the net premium tax credit, and amounts paid with an extension request.

Line 18.
Add the totals on line 16 and line 17 to compute total payments.

Line 19.
This represents your tax refund. A tax refund is due if the amount in line 18 is more than the amount on line 15.

Line 20.
If you want the refund due on line 19 deposited to your bank account, complete the info on line 20a and 20b.

Line 21.
You can have your tax refund applied to your next year's estimated taxes by completing the relevant information.

Line 22.
This represents tax you owe. Tax is owed if the amount in line 18 is less than the amount on line 15.

Line 23.
This represents any estimated tax penalty that you might be charged for failing to make estimated payments on time.

The New Schedules

As already mentioned, the new schedules to accompany the tax return of some taxpayers are designated by numbers instead of letters, and here's a quick overview of each new schedule.

Schedule 1 - *Additional Income and Adjustments to Income*
This includes items from such as business income, alimony received, capital gains or losses, and adjustments including educator expenses and student loan interest expense.

Schedule 2 - *Tax*

This includes items such as the tax on a child's unearned income (commonly called the kiddie tax), the alternative minimum tax, and any excess premium tax credit that must be repaid.

Schedule 3 - *Nonrefundable Credits*
This includes items such as the foreign tax credit, the credit for child and dependent care, the education credit, and the residential energy credit.

Schedule 4 - *Other Taxes*
This includes items such as household employment taxes, the health care individual responsibility payment (the individual mandate), the net investment income tax, and the additional Medicare tax.

Schedule 5 - *Other Payments and Refundable Credits*
This includes items such as estimated tax payments, the net premium tax credit, and amounts paid with an extension request.

Schedule 6 - *Foreign Address and Third Party Designee*
This provides taxpayers who have a foreign address a place to list their country, province, and postal code and provides all taxpayers with a place to list information for a third-party designee who can discuss the return with the IRS.

Filing Requirements

Not all individuals will be required to file a tax return. Some lower income individuals may not meet the minimum requirements to file. Whether you are required to file a tax return depends primarily on your gross income, your age, and also on your filing status. For tax year 2018, you are required to file a tax return if your gross income was at least the amount shown on the following chart.

Single
Under age 65..$12,000
Blind or over 65.....................................$13,600

Married filing jointly
Both spouses under 65............................$24,000
One spouse is blind or over 65................$25,300
Both spouses are blind or over 65...........$26,600

Married filing separately
Any age...$12,000

Head of household

Under 65...$18,000
Blind or over 65..$19,600

Qualifying widow(er)
Under 65...$24,000
Blind or over 65..$25,300

Nonresident aliens might also be required to file a tax return if any of the following conditions apply:

- They engage, or are considered to be engaged in a trade or business in the United States during the tax year.
- They had U.S. income on which the tax liability was not satisfied by the withholding of tax at source.
- They are a fiduciary for a nonresident alien or estate.

Nonresident aliens are required to file an income tax return using Form 1040NR.

There are several reasons why you may want to file a tax return even if you do not meet the minimum income requirements:

- If you had taxes withheld from your pay, you must file a tax return to receive a tax refund.
- If you qualify, you must file a return to receive the refundable Earned Income Tax Credit.
- If you are claiming education credits, you must file to be refunded the American Opportunity Credit.
- If you have a qualifying child but owe no tax, you can file to be refunded the Additional Child Tax Credit.
- If you qualify, you must file to claim the refundable Health Coverage Tax Credit.
- If you adopted a qualifying child, you must file to claim the Adoption Tax Credit.
- If you overpaid estimated tax or applied a prior year overpayment to this year, you must file to receive the refund.

Tax Rates for the 2018 Tax Year

The amount of tax an individual is liable for is a factor of, (a) the individual's taxable income, and (b) a specified tax rate that is determined by the individual's total taxable income. Basically, the greater your taxable income; the higher the rate of tax.

Under the TCJA these are the tax brackets for the following income ranges:

Married Filing Jointly

Tax Bracket	Thresholds
10%	$0 to $19,050
12%	$19051 to $77,400
22%	$77,401 to $165,000
24%	$165,001 to $315,000
32%	$315,001 to $400,000
35%	$400,001 to $600,000
37%	Over $600,000

Head of Household

Tax Bracket	Thresholds
10%	$0 to $13,600
12%	$13,601 to $51,800
22%	$51,801 to $82,500
24%	$82,501 to $157,500
32%	$157,501 to $200,000
35%	$200,001 to $500,000
37%	Over $500,000

Single

Tax Bracket	Thresholds
10%	$0 to $9,525
12%	$9,526 to $38,700
22%	$38,701 to $82,500
24%	$82,501 to $157,500
32%	$157,501 to $200,000
35%	$200,001 to $500,000
37%	Over $500,000

Married Filing Separately

Tax Bracket	Thresholds
10%	$0 to $9,525
12%	$9,526 to $38,700
22%	$38,701 to $82,500
24%	$82,501 to $157,500
32%	$157,501 to $200,000
35%	$200,001 to $300,000
37%	Over $300,000

Social Security and Medicare Rates

Social Security taxes are assessed on employees' income below $128,400. Medicare taxes are assessed on all income. The 2018 Social Security Tax Rates are as follows:

- For both employees and employers — the Social Security tax rate is 6.2 percent. The Medicare tax rate is 1.45 percent; and
- For self-employed taxpayers—the Social Security tax rate is 12.4 percent on income under $128,400 and the Medicare tax rate is 2.9 percent.

2 Choosing Your Filing Status

An individual's tax refund or tax liability depends primarily upon two variables: the individual's *filing status* and the taxable income. Choosing the correct filing status, therefore, is very important, and is really the first step that you take in ensuring that you will end up with an accurately prepared tax return. You need to appreciate this, because your filing status determines a number of very important things, such as; filing requirements, tax deductions, tax credits, tax rate, and ultimately, your correct tax refund or tax liability. In general, filing status depends on whether a taxpayer is considered unmarried or married, and this is determined based on your marital on the last day of the tax year.

You must choose from one of five filing statuses, and you must know which one is correct for you. The five filing statuses are: (a) Single, (b) Married Filing Jointly, (c) Married Filing Separately, (d) Head of Household, and (e) Qualifying Widow/Widower. If you discover that more than one filing status applies to you, you may choose the one that gives you the lowest tax rate.

Single

You are required to file Single if any of the following conditions apply to you:

- You are unmarried on the last day of the tax year.
- You are divorced or legally separated under a separate maintenance decree on the last day of the tax year.
- You are widowed before the first day of the tax year and have not remarried during the tax year.

You normally file Single if you do not qualify for any other filing status, but there are some exceptions to the above (see below), if you provide for a child living with you, or if you are a surviving spouse. In these cases you will not be required to file Single, as long as certain other conditions are met.

Filing Single generally attracts a higher tax rate and has a lower standard deduction than some of the other filing statuses.

Married Filing Jointly (MFJ)

Marital status is decided based on a person's marital status on December 31. If a couple is married on December 31 of the tax year; that couple may file a joint return for the year, regardless of when in the year they got married. Consequently, you can file Married Filing Jointly if you and your spouse meet any one of the following tests:

- You are married and living together on the last day of the tax year.
- You are married on the last day of the tax year and living apart, but are not legally separated under a decree of divorce or separate maintenance.
- Your spouse died during the year and you did not remarry during the year.
- You are living together in a common law union that is recognized by the state where you live, or in the state where the common law union began.

In order to file a joint return, both spouses are required to include all their income, exemptions, and deductions on the joint return, and use the same accounting period.

The MFJ filing status generally has the lowest rate of tax, and is the more favorable filing status for married couples.

If your spouse died during the tax year, and you remarried during the year, you may file MFJ with your new spouse. You deceased spouse's filing status, however, would have to be Married Filing Separately.

Note however, that a married couple is <u>not</u> required to file jointly; this is a matter of choice; they can file separate returns if they wish.

Note also, that to file MFJ, both spouses do not need to have income to file jointly, however, both spouses are responsible for the joint return, and both must sign the return.

Nonresident and Dual-Status Aliens

Generally, a joint return cannot be filed if either spouse was a nonresident alien at any time during the year. However, if at the end of the year one spouse was a nonresident alien or dual-status alien married to a U.S. citizen or resident, both spouses may choose to file a joint return. In this case, both spouses will be taxed as U.S. citizens and residents for the entire year, and the nonresident spouse must report <u>all</u> income (both domestic and foreign).

Annulled Marriages

If one spouse obtains a court decree of annulment (which holds that no valid marriage ever existed), both spouses must file amended returns claiming a filing status of Single or Head of Household, whichever applies, for all prior tax years affected by the annulment that are not closed by the statute of limitations.

Divorced Taxpayers

In the case of divorce, both spouses may be held jointly and individually responsible for any tax, interest, and penalties due on a joint return before the divorce. This responsibility applies even if the divorce decree states that only one spouse will be responsible for any amounts due on previously filed joint returns.

Married Filing Separately (MFS)

If you are married and decide not to file a joint return with your spouse, you must file Married Filing Separately.

There is, however, one exception to this rule: A married taxpayer can be considered unmarried by law, if he/she maintains a household for a child, and the spouse was not a member of the household for the last six months of the taxable year. Such a taxpayer would not be required to file MFS, but will be able to file as Head of Household (see below).

Although filing a joint return generally produces lower taxes, the opposite is sometimes the case, and to maximize the tax advantage in such circumstances, married couples may decide to file separately for a particular year. Married taxpayers, therefore, have the option of filing Married Filing Separately, and can consider this option if:

- Each spouse wants to be responsible for his/her taxes only.
- Both spouses agree not to file a joint return.

When you file MFS, you report only your own income, credits, and deductions. You should consider carefully before choosing this option, because Filing MFS usually puts you at a disadvantaged position, and usually means paying more taxes than filing MFJ. This is so because MFS has the highest tax rate. Filing MFS also disqualifies you from most of the credits/deductions that are available for the other filing statuses (see below). If you file MFS, you are required also to enter your spouse's full name and Social Security number on the tax return. Note that you can change a MFS return to a MFJ return within three years, by filing an amended return. You cannot change from MFJ to MFS however.

The Disadvantages of Filing Married Filing Separately

There are certain distinct disadvantages if you choose the MFS filing status that you should be aware of, and these are as follows:

- You <u>cannot</u> claim the standard deduction if your spouse itemizes; in this case, you must itemize also. This means then, that you could lose out on a substantial deduction if the expenses that you have to itemize are less than the amount of the standard deduction.
- You cannot claim the credit for child and dependent care expenses in most cases.
- You cannot claim the education credits, the deduction for student loan interest, or the tuition and fees deduction.
- You cannot claim the earned income credit.
- You cannot exclude from income any interest earned from Series EE U.S. Savings Bonds that was used for higher education expenses.
- You cannot claim the credit for adoption expenses in most cases.
- You may have a smaller child tax credit than if you filed jointly.
- Your capital loss deduction is limited to $1,500 (instead of $3,000 for all other filing statuses).

Also, if you lived with your spouse at any time during the year and filed MFS, you:
- Cannot claim the credit for the elderly or the disabled.
- May have to include more Social Security benefits received in taxable income.
- Cannot roll over amounts from a traditional IRA to a Roth IRA.

Head of Household (HOH)

If you are unmarried, on the last day of the tax year, you can file Head of Household if the following conditions apply:
(a) You paid more than half the costs of keeping up a home for the tax year, and
(b) A qualified person (see definition below) lived with you for more than half of the tax year.

Filing Head of Household can have substantial financial benefits over filing as a single status taxpayer. In filing as Head of Household, one enjoys lower tax rates and a larger Standard Deduction.

In determining the cost of keeping up a home, you may include costs such as mortgage interest, real estate tax, home insurance, repairs, utilities, and food. You cannot include amounts you paid for clothing, education, medical treatment, vacations, life insurance, transportation, or the rental value of your home. In determining the amount you paid in keeping up the house, you must exclude any payments received from public assistance.

Definition of a Qualifying Person

To choose the Head of Household filing status, the general rule is that you must have a qualifying person living with you for at least half of the year. A qualifying person includes any of the following:

- An unmarried child, including your own child, grandchild, stepchild, or foster child. The child does not necessarily have to be a dependent on your tax return, but must live with you. (For example, the child could be claimed by the other parent, but you would still be able to claim the Head of Household filing status, as long as the child lived with you.)
- A married child, including your own child, grandchild, stepchild, or foster child. In this case, the child must be a dependent on your tax return.
- A relative who is a dependent on your tax return, such as your parent, grandparent, brother, sister, stepbrother, stepsister, half-brother or half-sister, niece or nephew.

Parent Not Living With You

There is one exception to the rule that your dependent must live with you to qualify you for the Head of Household filing status. You can file as Head of Household even if your parent does not physically live with you, as long as you paid more than half the cost of keeping up a home that was the parent's main home for the entire year. For example, your parent could be living in a rest home or home for the elderly.

Temporary Absence

You and your qualifying person are still considered to live together even if one or both of you are temporary absent from the home, due to special circumstances such as illness, education, business, vacation, or military service.

Married Considered Unmarried

You can also file HOH if you are married but considered unmarried. This is a very important exception to the rule that married people who decide not to file a joint return together, must file Married Filing Separately. If you are married and separated from your spouse, under tax law you may be considered unmarried, if certain conditions are met. This means that you could qualify to file HOH instead of MFS, and will not be subject to the disadvantages of the MFS filing status.

Under tax law, you can be considered unmarried on the last day of the tax year if you meet all the following tests:

- You must file a separate return from your spouse.
- You must have paid more than half the costs of keeping up a home for the tax year.
- You must not have lived with your spouse at any time during the last 6 months of the tax year.
- Your home was the main home for your child, stepchild, or eligible foster child for more than half of the year.
- You must be able to claim an exemption for the child. You still meet this test if the child was not claimed because you allowed the non-custodial parent to claim the exemption for the child.

Other Points to Consider

Note that a person, who is your qualifying relative, ONLY because he or she lived with you as a member of your household (no blood or marriage relationship) for the entire year, CANNOT qualify you for the HOH filing status. For example: a live-in boyfriend or girlfriend, or boyfriend's or girlfriend's child does not qualify you for HOH. Neither does a cousin qualify you for HOH.

Qualifying Widow/Widower with Dependent Child (QW)

Surviving spouses receive the same standard deduction and tax rates as taxpayers who are filing Married Filing Jointly. In the year of your spouse's death, if you do not remarry, you can file a joint return with your deceased spouse. For the following two years, you can use the Qualifying Widow/Widower with Dependent Child filing status, if you have a dependent child living with you. After two years, if you have not remarried, you must change your filing status to either Single or Head of Household, depending on your circumstances.

You can consider the Qualifying Widow(er) filing status if you are a widow(er) and:

- You could have filed a joint return with your spouse for the year your spouse died.
- Your spouse died in either of the two tax years preceding this current year.
- You have a child or stepchild who qualifies as a dependent. (Note that this does not include a foster child.)
- You paid over half the costs of keeping up a home for the entire year.
- The child lived in your home all year, except for periods of temporary absence.

Some Tax Planning Points

- If you and your spouse each have income, it might be wise to figure your taxes both on a joint return and on separate returns, and then choose the filing status that gives you the lower combined tax. Generally, you will pay more combined tax on separate returns than you would on a joint return, because the tax rate is higher for the MFS filing status. However, if both you and your spouse have large incomes; and both of you also have large deductions, there may be a possibility that filing MFS could result in lower tax, as separating the incomes will place you both in a lower tax bracket.

-
- If your spouse dies during the year and has a tax liability, for example, because there was not enough tax withheld for his or her salary, you might want to consider filing MFS. If you file MFJ you will be responsible for the entire tax.

- Remember, you may qualify to file HOH if you are single, and support your parent who is in a retirement or nursing home.

- Since each filing status has its own tax rate and its own standard deduction, you can choose to file under a different filing status each year, if you qualify to do so.
- Remember, also, that if you are married but separated, you may file HOH, but you and your spouse must be living in separate places. Living in the same house under "emotional estrangement" does not qualify as living apart for HOH purposes.

3 The Standard Deduction vs. Itemized Deductions

In preparing your tax returns, you are allowed the choice of either claiming the standard deduction, or claiming itemized deductions. Your deductions (standard or itemized) are subtracted from your adjusted gross income (AGI) to figure your taxable income. Depending on which choice gives you the greater benefit, you may choose to take your standard deduction, or you may choose to claim itemized deductions; the aim here is to maximize your refund or minimize your tax liability. The objective, then, is to provide you with relevant knowledge to enable you to make an informed decision whether you should take the standard deduction or whether you should claim itemized deductions.

Defining the Standard Deduction

The standard deduction is a fixed dollar amount that the government allows taxpayers who do not itemize deductions to deduct from their income. The standard deduction reduces the amount of income that is taxed, and eliminates the need for many taxpayers to itemize deductions, because you can take the higher deduction of the two. This deduction is based on your filing status, and is available to U.S. citizens and resident aliens. It is not available to nonresident aliens residing in the United States.

The Standard Deduction may also include additional amounts for age and blindness.

The amount of your standard deduction generally depends on the following:

- Your filing status.
- Whether you are 65 or older and/or blind. (Your standard deduction is higher if you are over 65 years old, and/or blind.)
- Whether you can be claimed as a dependent on another person's tax return.

For tax year 2018, the new standard deduction amounts under the TCJA for the various filing statuses are as follows:

- Single - $12,000
- MFJ - $24,000
- MFS - $12,000
- HOH - $18,000
- QW - $24,000

Elderly and/or blind taxpayers receive an additional standard deduction amount added to the basic standard deduction. The additional standard deduction for a blind taxpayer (a taxpayer whose vision is less than 20/200) and for a taxpayer who is age 65 or older at the end of the year is $1,300 for married individuals; and $1,600 for singles and heads of household.

The additional standard deduction is doubled for taxpayers who are both age 65 and blind.

You are not eligible to claim the standard deduction if any of the following situations apply to you:

- You and your spouse use the Married Filing Separately filing status, and your spouse itemizes deductions. In this case, you cannot claim the standard deduction, but must also itemize deductions.
- You are filing for a short year, due to a change in your annual accounting period.
- You were a nonresident or a dual-status alien during the year.

If you can be claimed as a dependent on another person's tax return, your standard deduction is limited to the greater of: (a) $1,050, or (b) your total earned income for the year plus $350 (but not exceeding $12,000 the standard deduction for the dependent's filing status.)

Defining Itemized Deductions

You should itemize deductions if your total eligible expenses are more than the standard deduction amount. Also, you must itemize if you do not qualify for the standard deduction. Itemized deductions are comprised of certain eligible expenses that individual taxpayers in the United States can report on their federal income tax returns in order to decrease their taxable income. Most taxpayers are allowed a choice between the itemized deductions and the standard deduction.

To claim your itemized deductions, you must complete Schedule A, Itemized Deductions. You enter all your eligible expenses in the appropriate sections on Schedule A, which your tax preparation software will transfer to your tax return.

Note that prior tax law placed an overall limitation on certain itemized deductions applicable to higher income individuals whose adjusted gross income (AGI) exceeds specified limits based on the taxpayer's filing status. The TCJA has suspended the overall limitation on itemized deductions for tax years beginning after December 31, 2017 through December 31, 2025.

Accordingly, itemized deductions are not reduced for higher-income taxpayers.

The eligible expenses that you are allowed to claim on Schedule A, fall into the following broad categories:

- Medical and dental expenses.
- State and local taxes you paid.
- Home mortgage interest you paid
- Gifts to charity.
- Casualty and theft losses.

Deducting Medical and Dental Expenses

The medical and dental expense deduction is subject to an AGI threshold, and only unreimbursed medical and dental expenses that exceed the threshold may be deducted.

Generally, you can claim a deduction for medical and dental expenses you incurred, but only to the extent that they exceed 10% of your adjusted gross income (AGI). For example, your AGI is $50,000 and your medical expenses total $6,000. Since 10% of $50,000 is $5,000, you can only take a deduction of $1,000 (6,000-5,000). The TCJA, however, reduced the applicable threshold for the deduction of unreimbursed medical and dental expenses to 7.5% of AGI for the years 2017 and 2018, but for 2019 onwards it reverts back to the 10% threshold.

The criteria for applying this restriction, from the government's perspective, is for the IRS to prevent taxpayers with large salaries from claiming expenses they can certainly afford, as tax deductible items, while benefiting lower income taxpayers who are burdened by unforeseen medical costs.

You can include medical expenses for yourself and your spouse, your dependents claimed on your return, and others you could have claimed as a dependent, except that they didn't meet the gross income test, or they filed a joint return.

Deductible Medical Expenses

Not all medical expenses that you incur are deductible. Medical and dental expenses are eligible only if they were paid for the prevention or relief of a physical defect, mental defect, or illness. You can claim expenses paid for treatment, diagnosis, cure, or the prevention of disease.

Deductible medical expenses include the following:

- Doctors, dentists, and other medical practitioners' fees.
- Hospital services fees (lab work, therapy, surgery, etc.)
- Prescription medicine.
- Meals and lodgings provided by a hospital during medical treatment (see below for more details).
- The cost and care of guide dogs or animals aiding the blind.
- The cost of lead-based paint removal.
- The expenses of an organ donor.
- Long-term care contracts.
- Transportation expenses for medical care (see below for more details).
- Wages paid for nursing services.
- Treatment in a drug or alcohol center (includes meals and lodging).
- Legal abortion.
-
- The cost of living in a retirement home (for yourself, your spouse, or your dependent) is deductible if any party was required to live there because of the availability of medical care.
-
- Medical insurance premiums for policies that cover medical and dental care (including hospital and surgical fees), prescription drugs, eyeglasses, replacement for contact lens, and qualified long-term care insurance contracts.

If you make improvements to your home that are required because of medical conditions, but which do not add value to your home, these costs can be deductible. These costs would include rails, wheel chair ramps, etc.

Amounts you incur for participating in a weight-loss program as treatment for a specific disease (including obesity) are deductible, if diagnosed by a physician.

You can deduct transportation expenses that you incur, as long as these expenses were incurred primarily for, and were essential to the medical care received.

The following rules apply to deductible medical transportation expenses:

- You can claim mileage at a standard rate of 18 cents per mile, or you can deduct the actual out of pocket expenses.
- You can deduct all tolls and parking fees incurred, whether you claim standard mileage or actual expenses.
- You cannot deduct depreciation, insurance, general repair, and maintenance expenses for your vehicle.
- Transportation is not only limited to your car expenses, but can also include expenses incurred for ambulance, bus, taxi, train, or plane.

- Transportation expenses include also amounts incurred for another person including a parent or a nurse, if the patient is unable to travel alone.
- You can deduct the costs of lodging and meals at a hospital or similar institution, if the main reason for being there is for medical care. To be deductible, the following must apply:

- The lodging must be primarily essential to medical care.
- A doctor must provide the medical care, and the care must be provided in a medical care facility.
-
- The lodging must not be extravagant.
- There must be no significant element of personal pleasure, recreation, or vacation in the travel away from home.
- Lodging expenses are limited to $50 per night per person.

Nondeductible Medical Expenses

Not all medical expenses are tax deductible. The IRS has compiled a list of medical expenses that cannot be deducted, and these expenses include the following:

- Health club dues.
- Household help.
- Social activities, such as dancing lessons (even if following doctor's advice).
- Stop smoking programs.
- Trips for general health improvement (even if following doctor's advice).
- Weight loss programs, unless for obesity or other disease.
- Illegal controlled substances.
- Life insurance or income protection policies; or policies providing for loss of life, limb, sight, etc.
- Cosmetic surgery (unless necessary to improve deformity arising from, or directly related to, a congenital deformity, a personal injury resulting from an accident or trauma, or a disfiguring disease).
- Nonprescription medicine.
- Maternity clothing.
- Health savings account payments for medical expenses.
- Teeth whitening.
- Toothpaste, toiletries, cosmetics, etc.
- Nursing care for a healthy baby.

If a taxpayer is reimbursed during the current tax year for medical expenses that were deducted on Schedule A in a prior year, then generally the amount reimbursed should be reported as income in the current year, up to the amount that was previously deducted as medical expenses.

Also, if you receive an amount in settlement of a damage suit for personal injuries, part of that award may be for future medical expenses. If it is, you must reduce any future medical expenses for these injuries until the amount you received has been completely used.

If you were self-employed and had a net profit for the year, you may be able to deduct, as an adjustment to income, amounts paid for medical and qualified long-term care insurance on behalf of yourself, your spouse, your dependents, and, your children who were under age 27 at the end of the tax year.

Some Other Points to Consider

- You can deduct medical expenses in the year you paid them, regardless of when the services were provided.
-
- If you are deducting medical expenses for your spouse, you must have been married at the time the expenses were incurred, or when they were paid.

- You can deduct medical expenses for a deceased spouse or dependent in the year they were paid.

- If both parents, who are divorced or separated, combine to provide more than half the child's support, either spouse can deduct medical expenses paid for the child.

- Amounts contributed to a medical savings account are not deductible as medical expenses. These amounts can be deducted as an adjustment to income on you tax return.

Deducting Taxes You Paid

State and local taxes paid by an itemizing taxpayer has generally been a deductible item on the taxpayer's federal income tax return without limit. The TCJA, however, now limits the federal income tax deduction for state and local taxes to $10,000 ($5,000 for married taxpayers filing separately) beginning in 2018.

Certain taxes you have already paid are allowable as itemized deductions. To be deductible, these taxes must have been imposed on you personally, and you must have paid them during the year.

The following taxes you paid during the year are deductible on Schedule A:

-
- State and local income taxes.
- Real estate taxes (deductible in the year you paid them).
- Personal property taxes charged on the value of personal property.
- Foreign income taxes paid.

The following taxes are not deductible:

- Federal income taxes.
- Employee contributions to private or voluntary disability plans.
- Trash or pickup fees.
- Federal excise taxes.
- Homeowner's association fees.
- Rent increase due to higher real estate taxes.
- Social Security and other employment taxes for household workers.
- Taxes for local benefits (e.g. property improvements).
- Transfer taxes.
- Gift taxes.
- Estate or inheritance taxes.
- Fines and penalties.

State and Local Income Taxes

You can deduct state and local income taxes paid. State and local income taxes withheld from your wages are reported to you in boxes 17 and 19 of Form W-2.

Real Estate Taxes

As a homeowner, you are entitled to deduct payments of real estate tax on your property if you claimed itemized deductions on your tax return. Deductible real estate taxes are generally any state, local, or foreign taxes on real property. They must be charged uniformly against all property in the jurisdiction and must be based on the assessed value. There are no limits on the dollar amount of real estate taxes you can deduct, and there are no limits on the number of homes for which you can claim the deduction.

Real estate taxes relating to property sold/purchased during the year must be divided between the seller and the buyer according to the number of days each owned the property during the property tax year. The real estate tax for each property bought or sold during the year is figured as follows:

- Divide the number of days the property was owned during the tax year by 365.

- Multiply the percentage calculated above by the total real estate taxes for the year.

If the buyer agrees to pay delinquent taxes, he or she cannot deduct them. He or she must add them to the cost of the property. The seller can deduct taxes paid by the buyer.

Personal Property Taxes

Deductible personal property taxes are taxes that are imposed, based on the value of personal property such as a boat or car. The tax must be charged to you on a yearly basis, even if it is collected more than once a year or less than once a year.

Foreign Income Taxes Paid

Generally, you can take either a deduction on Schedule A, or a tax credit for foreign income taxes imposed on you by a foreign country, or a United States possession. (Note that a credit is usually more valuable than a deduction, because a credit reduces tax on a dollar-for-dollar basis.)

Deducting Interest You Paid

Certain types of interest you pay are deductible as an itemized deduction. The types of interest you can deduct on Schedule A are home mortgage interest, points in some cases, and investment interest.

Home Mortgage Interest

The TCJA made the following changes to the existing home mortgage interest deduction for taxable years 2018 through 2025:
- Interest paid on home equity indebtedness—home equity loans and lines of credit, in other words—incurred after December 15, 2017 is not tax-deductible unless used to buy, build or substantially improve the taxpayer's home that secures the loan;

- Interest paid on acquisition debt incurred after December 15, 2017, less any acquisition debt incurred on or before December 15, 2017, is limited to interest paid on total acquisition indebtedness but only if the total of such mortgages is $750,000 or less ($375,000 or less if married filing separately).

- Interest paid on acquisition debt incurred on or before December 15, 2017 is limited to interest paid on acquisition indebtedness of $1,000,000 or less ($500,000 or less if married filing separately).

Home mortgage interest is the most common interest deduction on a typical Schedule A, and is any interest that you paid on a loan secured by a main home or a second home. To qualify for the home mortgage interest deduction, the following rules apply:

- You must be legally liable for the loan. Therefore, you cannot deduct interest payments you make for someone else if you are not legally liable to make those payments.
- Both you and the lender must intend that the loan be repaid. In addition, there must be a true debtor-creditor relationship between you and the lender.
- The mortgage must be a secured debt on a qualified home.
- You can only deduct interest paid on your main home and a second home. Interest paid on third or fourth homes, for example, is not deductible.
- Late payment charges and prepayment penalty on a mortgage are deductible as mortgage interest.

Your home mortgage interest is reported to you and the IRS on a Form 1098 by the lending institution.

Deducting Points
"Points" is the term used to describe certain charges paid to obtain a home mortgage. Points may be deductible as home mortgage interest if you itemize deductions on Schedule A. If you can deduct all of the interest on your mortgages, you may be able to deduct all of the points paid on the mortgage.

You may be able to deduct your points in full in the year they are paid, if all the following requirements are met:

- The loan is secured by your main home. (Your main home is the one you live in most of the time).
- Paying points is an established business practice in your area.
- The points paid are not more than the amount generally charged in that area.
- You use the cash method of accounting. (This means you report income in the year you actually receive it, and deduct expenses in the year you actually pay them.)
- The points were not paid for items that usually are separately stated on the settlement sheet, such as appraisal fees, inspection fees, title fees, attorney fees, or property taxes.
- The funds you provided at or before closing, plus any points the seller paid, were at least as much as the points charged. This means that you

cannot have borrowed the funds from your lender or mortgage broker in order to pay the points.
- You use the loan to buy or build your main home.
- The points were computed as a percentage of the principal amount of the mortgage.
- The amount is clearly shown as points on your settlement statement.

Points that do not meet all the above requirements cannot be fully deducted in the year paid, but can be amortized over the life of the loan.

Note also the following:

- Points paid on loans secured by a second home cannot be deductible in full in the year paid, but must be amortized over the life of the loan.
- If points are being deducted over the life of the mortgage, and the mortgage ends early, you can deduct any remaining balance in the year the mortgage ends.
- Points paid by the seller are deductible by the buyer. The buyer must however, reduce the basis (cost) of the home by the amount of seller-paid points.
- Points paid for refinancing, generally can only be deducted over the life of the new mortgage.
- Mortgage insurance premiums may also be deductible, but only as reported to you on Form 1098.

Points paid are usually reported to you on Form 1098, and you claim them on line 10 of your Schedule A, along with mortgage interest paid. Any points you paid that were not reported on Form 1098, can be claimed on line 12 of Schedule A.

Deducting Investment Interest

Investment interest expense is interest paid on money borrowed to buy property held for investment, such as interest on securities in a margin account. A taxpayer can deduct investment interest expense, but the deduction is limited to the taxpayer's net investment income. Investment interest expense incurred to produce tax-exempt income is not deductible. You can therefore, deduct investment interest only to the extent of net investment income. If you have excess investment interest that you cannot deduct, these can be carried over into future years when you have investment income to offset them against. You must use Form 4952, Investment Interest Expense Deduction, to figure the amount of deductible investment interest.

Deducting Business Interest

Business interest is not deductible on Schedule A as an itemized deduction, but can be deducted on Schedule C or C-EZ (see business section). There is no limit on the amount of business interest that can be deducted.

Nondeductible Interest

The following interest and related expenses are never deductible:

- Lender's appraisal fees.
- Preparation cost of loan papers.
- Settlement fees and notary fees.
- Service charges.
- Non-redeemable ground rent.
- Interest on income tax paid to the IRS or to a state or local tax agency.
- Annual fees on credit cards.
- Credit investigation fees.
- Interest relating to tax-exempt income.
- Interest to purchase or carry tax-exempt securities.
- Personal interest: car loans (non-business use), finance charges on credit cards and consumer loans, late payment charges by a utility.

Deducting Gifts to Charity

You may claim as an itemized deduction, any charitable contributions of money or property you made to qualified charitable organizations. Generally, you may deduct charitable contributions of up to 60% of your adjusted gross income, but 20% and 30% limitations may apply in some cases. You may deduct a charitable contribution made to, or for the use of, any organization that is qualified under the Internal Revenue Code.

Defining Charitable Organizations

A qualified charitable organization is a nonprofit organization that qualifies for tax-exempt status according to the U.S. Treasury. Qualified charitable organizations must be operated exclusively for religious, charitable, scientific, literary or educational purposes, or for the prevention of cruelty to animals or children, or the development of amateur sports. Contributions made to tax-exempt charitable organizations are eligible for tax deduction on federal income tax returns. IRS Publication 78 lists most organizations that qualify to receive tax-deductible contributions.

Qualified charitable organizations include the following:

- Churches, synagogues, and religious organizations.
- Salvation Army, Red Cross, CARE, Goodwill Industries, United Way, Boy and Girl Scouts, Boys and Girls Club of America, etc.
- War veterans' organizations.
- Nonprofit schools and hospitals.
- Federal, state, and local governments (but only if gifts are for public purposes).
- Civil defense organizations.
- Public parks and recreation facilities.
- Most nonprofit charitable organizations.
- Nonprofit volunteer fire companies.
- A nonprofit cemetery company, if the funds are irrevocably dedicated to the perpetual care of the cemetery as a whole, and not for a particular lot or mausoleum crypt.

What Charitable Contributions are Deductible?

Deductible charitable contributions include the following:

- Money.
- Dues and fees.
- Amounts paid to a qualified organization above the value of any benefits received from the organization in return.
- Used clothing, furniture, etc. The fair market values of these items are deductible, and the items must be in good used condition.
- Used vehicles, boats, and airplanes (see below).
- The cost and upkeep of uniforms worn while performing donated services. These uniforms however, must not be for general wear.
- Un-reimbursed transportation expenses that relate directly to the service to be performed for the qualified organization.
- The part of your contribution above fair market value for items such as merchandise, tickets, charity balls, or sporting events.

The following contributions are not deductible, and you cannot include them on Schedule A:

- Contributions to country clubs and other social clubs.
- Contributions to civic leagues, sports clubs, labor unions.
- Contributions to chamber of commerce and other business organizations.
- Tuition payments.
- Cost of raffle, bingo, or lottery tickets.
- Value of your time or services.
- Political contributions.
- Blood donated to a blood bank or to the Red Cross.

- Car depreciation, insurance, general repairs, or maintenance.
- Any contribution that is earmarked for the use of a specific individual.
- Sickness or burial expenses for members of a fraternal society.
- Part of a contribution that personally benefits you.
- Contributions made to groups that are run for personal profits.
- Contributions made to groups whose purpose is to lobby for law changes.
- Contributions to lobbyist groups.

If you give a deductible contribution and receive a benefit in return, you are allowed to deduct only the amount by which the contribution exceeds the fair market value of the benefit received.

To be deductible, the contributions must actually be paid in cash or other property before the close of your tax year, whether you use the cash or accrual method. It is very important that you keep proper records of all your cash and non-cash contributions.

Rules for Deducting Cash Contributions

You cannot deduct a cash contribution, regardless of the amount, unless you keep a record of the contribution. The following rules apply:

- For individual contributions under $250, your proof can be your canceled check or your receipt, or a bank statement containing the name of the charity, the date, and the amount.
- For individual contributions of $250 or more, you must obtain a written acknowledgement from the organization, as proof of the contribution. In figuring whether a contribution is $250 or more, you must not combine separate contributions to the same organization; each payment is treated as a separate contribution.
- A written acknowledgement for a contribution of $250 or more must be received before the due date of the tax return (including extensions) and must include: (a) the amount of the cash contribution, (b) whether the qualified organization gave you any goods or services in return for the contribution (other than certain token items and membership benefits), and (c) a description and good faith estimate of the value of any goods or services that were provided to you in return for the contribution.

General Rules for Deducting Non-Cash Contributions

Generally, non-cash charitable contributions are tax deductible at the fair market value (FMV) of the property contributed. The following rules apply to non-cash contributions:

41

- For donations of used cars, boats, airplanes, if you claim a value of $500 or more for any of these items, you must obtain a written acknowledgement from the organization. The deduction allowed is the smaller of the fair market value (FMV) on the date of the contribution, or the gross proceeds received from the sale of the item.
- For donated motor vehicles, a used car guide can be used to determine the FMV of the vehicle.
- You must file Form 8283, Noncash Charitable Contributions with your tax return if your total deduction for non-cash contributions for the year is over $500.

Rules for Deducting Non-Cash contributions Over $5,000

If you donate non-cash property valued at over $5,000 to a qualified organization, the following rules apply:

- If the value of the property (other than publicly traded securities) exceeds $5,000, a qualified appraisal of the property must be done.
- You must attach Form 8283 to the tax return to support the charitable deduction, and the donee must sign Part IV of Section B, Form 8283.
- The person who signs for the donee must be an official who is authorized to sign the donee's tax or information returns, or a person specifically authorized to sign by that official.
- The signature does not represent concurrence with the appraised value of the contributed property.
- A signed acknowledgement represents receipt of the property described on Form 8283 on the date specified on the form. The signature also indicates knowledge of the information reporting requirements on dispositions. A copy of Form 8283 must be given to the donee.

Donating Your Services

You cannot claim a deduction for the value of your services contributed to a qualified organization, including the value of lost income, while working as an unpaid volunteer. Some expenses incurred while working as a volunteer, however, are deductible if they are:

- Unreimbursed.
- Directly connected with the service.
- Solely attributable to the service.
- Not personal, living, or family expenses.

For example, you can deduct either your actual car expenses, or the standard rate of 14 cents per mile. You can deduct travel expenses only if there is no significant element of personal pleasure, recreation, or vacation in such travel.

Limits on the Charitable Contribution Deduction

As stated above, your charitable contribution deduction may be limited to a certain percentage of your adjusted gross income. The amount of the deduction may be limited to 60%, 30%, or 20% of your adjusted gross income, depending on the type of charitable organization.

In general, if you contribute cash or short-term capital gain property to a public charity, the contributions may be deducted up to 60% of your adjusted gross income, computed without regard to any net operating loss carry-backs.

If you contributed property that would have yielded a long-term capital gain in a sale, then the deduction for the contribution is limited to 30% of your adjusted gross income in the year of donation if the organization is a public charity, and limited to 20% if the organization is a private foundation.

If you make charitable contributions in excess of these limits, the excess can be carried over to the following tax year. Excess contributions can be carried over for a maximum of five years.

How to Deduct Casualty and Theft Losses

The tax treatment of personal casualty losses and thefts is changed under the TCJA. Pursuant to the TCJA, the itemized deduction for personal casualty and theft losses is temporarily limited in tax years 2018 through 2025 solely to losses attributable to federally declared disasters. Consequently, you can only deduct casualty and theft losses if they're brought about due to an event that's been declared a disaster by the U.S. president.

Generally, you may claim an itemized deduction for any casualty and theft losses you suffered, relating to your home, household items, and vehicles. If your property was covered by insurance, you can deduct casualty and theft losses only if you filed a timely claim for reimbursement. Also, you must reduce the loss suffered, by the amount of any reimbursement you receive or expect to receive.

To be able to claim the deduction for the loss or damage to your property:

- You must first determine whether the loss has resulted from a casualty or theft under the IRS rules.

- You must complete Form 4684, Casualty and Thefts, to figure the amount of the loss, and the amount of that loss that you can deduct.

Defining a Casualty

The tax code defines a casualty as damage, destruction, or loss of property resulting from an identifiable event that is sudden, unexpected, or unusual, and includes any of the following:

- Natural disasters (earthquakes, storms, hurricanes, floods, tornadoes, etc.)
- Fires (except deliberately caused by the taxpayer).
- Shipwrecks.
- Terrorist attacks.
- Vandalism.
- Car accidents.

Under IRS rules, a casualty loss does not include loss caused from the normal wear and tear, or progressive deterioration of your property. Therefore, you cannot claim a casualty loss deduction for damage caused by any of the following:

- Termites or moths.
- Diseases.
- Progressive deterioration (for example, damage from continuous use of property).
- Drought.
- Arson committed by or on behalf of the taxpayer.
- Damage caused by ordinary accidents or willful acts or negligence (for example broken china, or damage done by a family pet).

Defining a theft

Theft is defined by the tax code as the taking and removing of money or property with the intent to deprive the owner of it. The taking must be illegal under the law of the state where it occurred, and it must have been done with criminal intent. Theft includes crimes such as:

- Blackmail.
- Burglary.
- Larceny.
- Embezzlement or extortion.
- Kidnapping for ransom.
- Robbery.

The onus is on you, the taxpayer, to prove your casualty and theft losses. To effectively prove your casualty losses, you must keep records, which show all of the following:

- The type of casualty.
- The date the casualty occurred.
- Evidence that the loss was a direct result of the casualty.
- Evidence that you owned the property, or were contractually liable for the loss, if it was leased property.

To prove a theft loss, your records must show the following:

- The date you discovered the property missing.
- Evidence that the property was stolen (a police report).
- Evidence that you were the owner of the property.

Figuring the Amount of the Loss

To determine the amount of loss you need to do two calculations:

- You first must calculate the adjusted basis of your property. The adjusted basis is usually the *original cost of the property plus the* cost of improvements, minus depreciation, and any previous casualty losses claimed.
- You must then calculate the decrease in fair market value of the property caused by the casualty or theft (see below).
-
- The smaller of these two calculations (adjusted basis or the decrease in fair market value) is the amount of your loss. From this amount, you must subtract any insurance settlement or reimbursement you receive or expect to receive.
-
- The decrease in fair market value is the difference between the value of the property immediately before, and immediately after the casualty or theft occurred. To figure the decrease in fair market value, you generally will need to have an appraisal done. You can however, use the cost of cleanup and repairs to measure the decrease in fair market value if:
- The repairs were necessary to bring the property back to its original condition before the casualty.
- The amount spent for the repairs is not excessive.

- The repairs were done <u>only</u> to take care of the damage caused by the casualty.
- The repairs do not increase the value of the property to more than its value before the casualty.

Figuring the Deduction

You can deduct a theft loss only in the year you discover the theft, and a casualty loss only in the year the casualty occurs, but you must first figure your allowable deduction for the year.

Casualty and theft losses <u>cannot</u> be deducted in full. In figuring your allowable deduction, you must first reduce your losses by any salvage value and any insurance or other reimbursement. The TCJA does not change the two limitations imposed by IRC section 165(h). The first limitation is a $100 floor per casualty event, meaning that only the loss amount in excess of $100 is deductible. The second limitation is a 10% of-adjusted-gross-income (AGI) floor, which applies to the total of the taxpayer's net casualty losses for the year after subtracting insurance reimbursements and the $100 dollar per event limitation.

For example, you have AGI of $20,000 and you suffered loss of $5,000 to your property, caused by a fire. You must first of all reduce the $5,000 loss by $100, which will leave you with $4,900. But this will further have to be reduced by $2,000 (10% of $20,000) to give you a deductible loss of $2,900.

How to Claim the Deduction for Property Covered by Insurance

If your property is covered by insurance, you <u>must</u> file a timely insurance claim for reimbursement of the loss. If you do not file a claim, you <u>cannot</u> take a deduction for casualty or theft losses. However, this rule does not apply to the portion of the loss not covered by insurance (for example, a deductible). You must reduce your loss by the amount of any insurance reimbursement you receive or expect to receive, even if you will not receive it until a later tax year. If your reimbursement is more than the basis (cost) in the property, you will have a capital gain, which must be reported in your income. You report a capital gain on Schedule D.

How to Claim for Losses on Deposits Held in Insolvent Financial Institutions

If you suffered a loss on deposits you had with an insolvent financial institution, you have three choices of how to deduct the loss:

- You can treat the loss as a non-business bad debt, and deduct it as a short-term capital loss on Schedule D.
- You can deduct the loss as a casualty loss on Schedule A.

Note that you cannot take a loss deduction for any part of the loss that is federally insured. If any loss deducted in a previous year is subsequently recovered, you must include the recovered amount in your current year income.

How to Claim Losses from Ponzi-Type Investment Schemes

If you suffered losses from a Ponzi-type investment scheme, these losses can be deducted as theft losses of income-producing properties in the year the loss is discovered. The loss is figured in Section B of Form 4684.

How to Claim Your Employee Business Expenses

Taxpayers who itemize their deductions formally have been able to deduct certain expenses as miscellaneous itemized deductions on schedule A to the extent that, in the aggregate, they exceed 2% of the taxpayer's AGI. Such taxpayer expenses included unreimbursed employee expenses, tax preparation fees, and certain other expenses. Under the TCJA, these miscellaneous itemized deductions subject to the 2% of AGI floor are suspended for expenses incurred after December 31, 2017 through 2025. In other words, you can NO longer deduct your employee business expenses.

Deductions Not Subject to the 2% of AGI Limitation

Deductible miscellaneous expenses were previously grouped into two separate categories those subject to the 2% of AGI limitation, which are no longer deductible, and those not subject to the 2% limitation, which are still deductible in full. These are claimed on line 28 of Schedule A, and include the following:

- Amortizable premium on taxable bonds.
- Casualty and theft losses from income-producing property.
- Federal estate tax on income in respect of a decedent.
- Gambling losses (but only to the extent of gambling winnings).
- Impairment-related work expenses of persons with disabilities.
- Loss from other activities from Schedule K-1.
- Repayment of more than $3,000 under a claim of right.
- Un-recovered investment in an annuity.

4 Claiming All Your Tax Credits

Millions of taxpayers overpay on their taxes every year, simply because they do not take advantage of all the tax credits that they are entitled to. Overlooking some of your tax credits can be a very costly mistake. Claiming all the credits that you are legally entitled to will allow you to save money, because credits reduce your tax liability on a dollar-for-dollar basis.

At this point, it should be pretty useful to make a distinction between adjustments to income and credits.

- Adjustments to income
- Adjustments are subtracted from your total income, to determine your adjusted gross income (AGI).

- Tax credits
- Tax credits reduce your tax liability on a dollar-for-dollar basis. A tax credit is generally much more valuable than an adjustment, because the tax credit directly reduces the actual amount of tax that must be paid. A deduction, on the other hand, only reduces the taxable income.

Tax credits are basically of two types: nonrefundable tax credits and refundable tax credits. Nonrefundable tax credits can reduce tax owed to zero, but you won't get a tax refund for the amount of the credit that exceeds the tax. Refundable credits, on the other hand, after they reduce your tax to zero, you will receive a refund for the amount that exceeds the tax. Most credits, however, both nonrefundable and refundable, are gradually reduced as your income increases, and are eventually phased out and reduced to zero after your income surpasses a certain level.

Defining Nonrefundable Credits

A nonrefundable tax credit is a credit that can reduce the amount of an individual's tax liability to zero, but cannot exceed the total amount of income taxes owed. In other words, you would not receive a tax refund if the credit exceeds the amount of your tax liability. For example, if you have a nonrefundable tax credit of $5,000 and a tax liability of $3,000, the credit will eliminate the tax liability, that is, reduce it to zero. The remaining $2,000 of the credit, however, will be lost, because the IRS will not send you a refund for this amount.

Nonrefundable credits for 2018 include the following:

- Credit for child and dependent care expenses.
- Child tax credit.
- Education credits.
- Residential energy credit.
- Foreign tax credit.
- Credit for the elderly and disabled.
- Credit for qualified alternative vehicles.
- Retirement saver's tax credit.
- Adoption credit

Defining Refundable Credits

A refundable tax credit, on the other hand, is not limited by the amount of an individual's tax liability, but can go beyond that and reduce an individual's tax liability below zero, and this will result in a tax refund. In other words, you would receive a tax refund if the credit exceeds the amount of your tax liability. For example, if you have a refundable tax credit of $5,000 and a tax liability of $3,000, the IRS would refund you the amount by which the tax credit exceeds the tax liability. You would therefore receive a tax refund of $2,000. Refundable credits can reduce tax liability to zero, and result in a refund of the amount by which the credits are greater than the tax liability, meaning, that the total amount of your refundable credits is refundable to you, even if there is no tax liability, or no taxes were withheld from your income.

Refundable credits for 2018 include the following:

- Earned income credit.
- Additional child tax credit.
- American opportunity credit (40% of the amount).
- Net premium tax credit.

The Child Tax Credit

The child tax credit is a credit given for each dependent child on your tax return, who is under the age of 17 at the end of the tax year. The child tax credit is a nonrefundable credit, and is intended to provide an extra measure of tax relief for taxpayers with qualifying children.

How to Qualify for the Child Tax Credit

To qualify for this credit, you must have a qualifying child on your tax return. The rules for determining if your child is a qualifying child for the purpose of this credit are as follows:

- The child must be your son, daughter, adopted child, stepchild, eligible foster child, brother, sister, stepbrother, stepsister, or a descendant of any of them. (This includes your niece, nephew, grandchild, great-grandchild, etc.)
- The child must not provide for over half of his or her own support for the year.
- The child must be a citizen or resident of the United States.
- The child must be under the age of 17 on the last day of the tax year.
- Generally, you must claim the child as a dependent on your tax return.
- The child must have lived with you for more than half of the year.
- The child must be younger than you.
- The child must not have filed a joint return, unless the joint return was filed only to claim a tax refund, and no tax liability would have existed on separate returns.

An adopted child qualifies be your qualifying child, even if the adoption is not final, as long as the child has been placed with you by an authorized agency for legal adoption.

An eligible foster child qualifies to be your qualifying child, as long as he or she was placed with you by an authorized placement agency, by judgment decree, or any other court of competent jurisdiction.

How to Claim the Child Tax Credit

Under the TCJA the child tax credit allows you to claim up to $2,000 per qualifying child. If you cannot claim the entire amount of the credit, because your tax is lower than the credit, and cannot absorb the full amount of the credit, you may be able to claim the balance as a refundable Additional Child Tax Credit (see below).

The Phase Out Amounts

The child tax credit is one of those credits, which begin to phase out after your income exceeds a certain amount. Under the TCJA, this credit begins to phase out when your modified adjusted gross income exceeds the following amounts for each filing status:

- MFJ - $400,000

- HOH, QW, or Single - $200,000
- MFS - $200,000

The Additional Child Tax Credit

If a child tax credit is reduced because of the taxpayer' tax liability that is lower than the credit to which the taxpayer would otherwise be eligible, the additional child tax credit may be payable as a refundable credit. The additional child tax credit is a credit for certain individuals who get less than the full amount of the child tax credit. Unlike the child tax credit, the additional child tax credit is a refundable tax credit and is available for up to $1,400.

The Credit for Child and Dependent Care Expenses

You may be able to claim a credit for child and dependent care, if you pay someone to care for your dependent child who is under the age of 13, or for your spouse or other dependent who is not able to care for himself or herself. You must have incurred this expenditure so that you (and your spouse, if you are married) could work or look for work. If you are married, both you and your spouse must have some form of earned income, unless one spouse either was a full-time student for 5 months of the tax year, or was physically or mentally incapable of self-care.

The child and dependent care credit, which is a nonrefundable credit, is generally a percentage of the amount of the work-related child and dependent care expenses you paid to a care provider. The amount of this percentage depends on your adjusted gross income.

Defining Work-Related Expenses

The tax credit for child and dependent care expenses is intended only to assist those who incur these expenses in order to enable them to earn income. Therefore, you can only claim dependent care expenses that the IRS considers to be work-related. Dependent care expenses incurred are considered work-related only if they are: (a) incurred to allow the taxpayer to work or look for work, and (b) are for a qualifying person's care.

Qualifying work-related expenses include the following:

- Household services, if they are at least partly responsible for the well-being and protection of a qualifying person. These can include cleaning service, maid, cook, and housekeeper's wages, room and board.

51

- Day care centers, if the center complies with all state and local regulations.
- Schooling, if the child is in a grade below the first grade and the amount paid cannot be separated from the cost of care.

Defining Qualifying Persons

For you to claim child and dependent care expenses, your qualifying person must be one of three types:

- A child under age 13 when the care was provided, and whom you can claim as a dependent on your tax return.
- Your spouse who was physically or mentally incapable of self-care.
- Your dependent who was physically or mentally incapable of self-care. To claim this credit, the qualifying person must have lived with you for more than half of the year. (There are exceptions for the birth or death of a qualifying person, or for a child of divorced or separated parents.)

The Requirements for Claiming the Credit

To be eligible to claim the credit, the expenses incurred must be for the qualifying person's well-being and protection; for example, placing your child in a day care center while you work or look for work.

To claim the credit, the following conditions must apply:

- The expenses incurred must be for the care of one or more qualified persons.
- You (and your spouse, if filing a joint return) must have some form of earned income from work performed during the year. Earned income includes employee compensation and net earnings from self-employment.
- If only one spouse has earned income, the IRS allows the other spouse to be treated as having earned income for any month he or she is: (a) a full time student (that is, a student for some part of each of 5 calendar months during the year), or (b) physically or mentally incapable of self-care (see below).
- The care must have been provided for the qualifying person so that you (and your spouse) can work or look for work.
- You must be paid for the work (must have earned income).
- Work also includes the process of actively looking for work, as long as you have some form of earned income during the year.
- The expenses for the care cannot be paid to any of the following persons: (a) your spouse, (b) the parent of your qualifying person, (c) someone you can claim as your dependent on your tax return, or (d)

your child who will not be age 19 or older by the end of the year, even if he or she is not your dependent.

- Your filing status must be Single, MFJ, HOH, or QW. You cannot claim this credit if you are filing MFS.
- You must identify the care provider on your tax return (see below).

A spouse who is either a full-time student, or who is not capable of self-care, is treated by the IRS as having earned income of $250 per month if there is one qualifying person, or $500 per month if there are two or more qualifying persons. This provision qualifies you to claim the credit even though your spouse has no earned income.

Figuring the Amount of the Credit

The amount of the work-related expenses that is eligible for the credit is limited to the <u>lowest </u>of these three amounts:

- The actual expenses you incurred.
- A dollar limit of $3,000 for one qualifying person; or $6,000 for two or more qualifying persons.
- Your earned income. (If you are filing a joint return, the earned income that you will use to do this comparison cannot be more than the smaller of each spouses' earned income.)

The qualifying expenses that you use to figure the credit must be reduced by the amount of any dependent care benefits provided by your employer that you exclude from your income. These amounts are shown in box 10 of your Form W-2.

The actual amount of the credit you receive is a percentage of the eligible work-related expenses you incurred. This ranges between 20% and 35% of your qualifying expenses, depending on your adjusted gross income, with the percentage decreasing as your income increases. For adjusted gross income above $43,000, the maximum credit you can claim is 20% of eligible expenses. Therefore, if you earn over $43,000, the maximum you can receive for this credit is $1,200 (20% of $6,000).

How to Claim the Credit

To claim the credit for child and dependent care expenses, you need to fill out Parts I and II of Form 2441, Child and Dependent Care Expenses. This form requires you to provide identification information (SSN or EIN) for the care provider(s) and the Social Security numbers of the qualifying children or disabled persons. The form helps you to compute your credit by comparing your allowable expenses with your wages and other earnings (and those of your spouse, if filing jointly). The amount of the credit, as figured on line 11 of Form 2441.

If your employer provided you with dependent care benefits, you must report this amount (which is shown in box 10 of your W-2) by completing Part III of Form 2441.

(Easily available off the shelf tax software will bring up Form 2441 for you to populate with the appropriate information, and the software will compute the amount to be included in your tax return.)

Note however, that if the information on Form 2441 is incomplete or incorrect, the IRS can disallow the credit, unless you can show due diligence in trying to provide the information.

Other Points to Consider

- You cannot claim work-related expenses paid for child and dependent care while you are off work due to illness. This applies even if you receive sick pay and is still considered an employee.
-
- You cannot claim transportation costs of getting a qualified person from home to the care location and back; this is not considered work-related expenses.

- If you pay someone to come to your home and care for your dependent or spouse, you may be considered a household employer, and may have to withhold and pay Social Security and Medicare tax, and also federal unemployment tax.

The Earned Income Credit

The earned income credit (EIC) is a tax credit that is specifically designed for lower income working families and individuals. The amount of the credit varies depending on your level of income and how many dependents you support. You can claim this credit with or without qualifying children, but greater tax credit is given to those who have qualifying children. This credit can be valued at over $6,000 if you have three or more qualifying children. The earned income credit is a refundable credit, which means that you will receive a tax refund whether or not you had any taxable income.

As the name implies, the earned income credit is provided as an incentive for individuals to work. Consequently, to qualify for this credit, you must have some form of earned income during the year. Earned income includes wages you get from working, and income you earn from self-employment.

Defining Earned Income

The types of earned income that will qualify you for the earned income credit includes the following:

- Wages, salaries, and tips.
- Net earnings from self-employment.
- Gross income received as a statutory employee.
- Nontaxable combat pay (if the taxpayer elects to include it in earned income). You are given the choice to elect to have your nontaxable combat pay included in earned income for purposes of claiming the earned income credit. Your nontaxable combat pay is reported in box 12 of your Form W-2, with the code "Q".
- Long-term disability benefits. Disability benefits received from an employer's disability retirement plan are considered earned income until you reach minimum retirement age.

The following income is not considered earned income when figuring the earned income credit:

- Interest and dividends.
- Pension and annuities.
- Social Security and retirement benefits.
- Alimony and child support.
- Welfare benefits.
- Worker's compensation and unemployment compensation.
- Employee compensation that is nontaxable while taxpayer is an inmate.

Who Can Claim the Earned Income Credit?

To be eligible to claim the earned income credit, both your **earned income** and your **adjusted gross income** must be within certain ranges (see below). The amount of the credit varies, based on your earned income and on how many qualifying children you are supporting in your household. Note also, that you may qualify for this credit even if you do not have a qualifying child.

The following rules apply when claiming the earned income credit:

- You, your spouse (if married filing jointly), and your qualifying children must have valid Social Security numbers.
- You must have some form of earned income, either from employment or from self-employment. If you are married, at least one spouse must work and have earned income.

- You must be a U.S. citizen or resident alien all year. A nonresident alien married to a U.S. citizen or resident alien, and filing a joint return, may also claim the credit.
- You <u>cannot</u> claim the credit if you are married, and your filing status is MFS.
- You ***cannot*** claim the credit if you are a qualifying child of another person.
- You cannot claim the credit if you file Form 2555 or 2555-EZ (relating to foreign earned income).
- You cannot claim the credit if your investment income for 2018 exceeds $3,500. (Investment income includes taxable and nontaxable interest income, dividend income, and net capital gains income).

Claiming the EIC with Qualifying Children

You will not be eligible to claim the credit if your qualifying child is also the qualifying child of another person with a higher AGI.

For your qualifying child to make you eligible to claim the credit, he or she must meet <u>all</u> of the following four tests:

(a) Relationship test: The child must be related to you by birth, marriage, adoption, or foster arrangement. Consequently, the child can be your son, daughter, stepchild, eligible foster child, brother, sister, stepbrother, stepsister, or a descendant of any of the above. An eligible foster child must be a child placed with you by an authorized agency.

(b) Age test: The child must be: (a) under 19 at the end of the year, (b) under 24 at the end of the year, <u>and</u> a full time student, or (c) permanently and totally disabled at any time during the tax year regardless of age.

(c) Joint return test: The child must not have filed a joint return with their spouse, unless filing <u>only</u> for a tax refund, and would have no tax liability if separate returns were filed.

(d) Residency test: The qualifying child must live with you in the United States for more than half of the year (12 months for a foster child).

Note that a qualifying child cannot be used by more than one person to claim the EIC. If two or more persons can claim the same qualifying child, both persons must choose between themselves who will claim the credit. If they cannot agree who will claim the child as a qualifying child, the IRS will apply the tiebreaker rules.

Claiming the EIC Without Qualifying Children

You can claim the earned income credit even if you do not have a qualifying child, but the following rules apply:

- You must be over 25 years old, but less than 65 years old at the end of the tax year. (If filing MFJ, only one spouse needs to meet the age test.)
- You (and your spouse, if filing a joint return) cannot be a dependent on another person's tax return.
- You cannot be a qualifying child of another person.
- You must have lived in the United States for more than half of the year.

How to Figure the Credit

The amount of earned income credit you can claim depends on a number of factors, which include your income, your filing status, and whether you have: (a) no qualifying children, (b) one qualifying child, (c) two qualifying children, or (d) three or more qualifying children.

For tax year 2018, to qualify for the EIC, <u>both</u> your **earned income** and **modified adjusted gross income** must be less than:

- $15,270 ($20,950 for married filing jointly) if you do <u>not</u> have a qualifying child.
- $40,320 ($46,010 for married filing jointly) if you have one qualifying child.
- $45,802 ($51,492 for married filing jointly) if you have two qualifying children.
- $49,194($54,884 for married filing jointly) if you have more than two qualifying children?

The maximum amount of credit for Tax Year 2018 is:

- $6,431 with three or more qualifying children
- $5,716 with two qualifying children
- $3,461 with one qualifying child
- $519 with no qualifying children

How to Claim the Credit

Because of the potential magnitude of this credit, the IRS pays a lot of attention to taxpayers who claim the earned income credit. This is because of the high incidence of fraudulent returns taxpayers have prepared to benefit from this credit. Consequently, if you wish to claim this credit, you must comply with the following requirements:

- Answer the earned income credit eligibility questions.
- Complete the Earned Income Credit Worksheet.
- If you have qualifying children, you must complete Schedule EIC, Earned Income Credit, and attach it to your tax return.

(Easily available off the shelf tax software will facilitate the completion of the above worksheets and schedules, and will figure the amount of the credit for inclusion on your tax return.)

To claim the earned income credit, you **must** file a tax return; you must do so even if you did not earn enough money that would require you to file a return. Because of the nature and potential value of this credit, the IRS may ask you to provide documents to prove that you are entitled to the earned income credit. These may include birth certificates, school records, medical records, etc., so it would be wise to have these handy.

Net Premium Tax Credit

Under the Affordable Care Act, if you purchase health insurance coverage through the Marketplace, you may be eligible for the Premium Tax Credit (PTC), which is a refundable credit, and which available to people with moderate incomes. Any advance payments (subsidy) made to the insurance company during the year are subtracted from the Premium Tax Credit calculated on the tax return, and the Net Premium Tax Credit credited on your tax return. Those who choose advance credit payments must complete Form 8962, and file a tax return to reconcile their advance credit payments with their actual Premium Tax Credit, even if they have gross income that is below the income tax filing threshold.

The Credit for Excess Social Security Tax

There is a maximum amount of wages that is subject to Social Security tax, and a maximum amount of tax that should be withheld. If you worked for two or more employers, the possibility exists that collectively too much Social Security or tier 1 Railroad Retirement (RRTA) tax could have been withheld from your wages. If this happens, you can claim any excess amount withheld, as a tax credit. Note however, that if any one employer erroneously withholds more than the maximum amount; you cannot claim the credit on your tax return; instead, that employer must repay this amount to you.

The Foreign Tax Credit

The foreign tax credit is intended to reduce the double taxation burden that would otherwise arise when foreign source income is taxed by both the United States and the foreign country from which the income is derived.

Four tests must be met to qualify for the credit:

- The tax must be imposed on you.
- You must have paid or accrued the tax.
- The tax must be a legal and actual foreign tax liability, and
- The tax must be an income tax.

You can choose either to deduct foreign taxes paid on Schedule A, as an itemized deduction, or you can take the foreign tax credit. The foreign tax credit is a nonrefundable credit.

You cannot take a deduction or credit for foreign taxes paid on income that you excluded from U.S. tax under any of the following:

- Foreign earned income exclusion.
- Foreign housing exclusion.
- Income from Puerto Rico exempt from U.S. tax.
- Possession exclusion.
- Extraterritorial income exclusion.

You generally claim the foreign tax credit by filing Form 1116, Foreign Tax Credit. You can however, claim the foreign tax credit **without** using Form 1116 if all of the following requirements are met:

- You are an individual.
- Your only foreign income source is passive income (interest, dividends, royalties, etc.)
- The foreign tax for the year is not more than $300 ($600 if filing a joint return).
- You elect this procedure for the tax year.

The Adoption Credit

You may qualify for the adoption credit if you adopted or attempted to adopt a child in 2018, and paid qualified expenses relating to the adoption. The credit is valued at up to $13,840 for each effort to adopt an eligible child. The effort ends when the child is adopted. For 2018, the adoption credit is a nonrefundable credit.

Defining Qualified Adoption Expenses

Qualified adoption expenses are all expenses that are directly related to, and whose principal purpose is for the legal adoption of a child. These expenses include the following:

- Adoption fees.
- Court fees.
- Attorney fees.
- Travel expenses (including amounts spent for meals and lodging) while away from home.
- Expenses to adopt a foreign child.

The following are not considered qualified adoption expenses, and cannot be deducted:

- Expenses that violate state or federal law.
- Expenses incurred for carrying out a surrogate parenting arrangement.
- Expenses for the adoption of a spouse's child.
- Amounts for which you received funds under any federal, state, or local program.
- Amounts, which are allowed as a credit or deduction under any other federal income tax rule.
- Amounts paid or reimbursed by an employer, or other person or organization.
- Any amounts paid before 1997.

How to Claim the Adoption Credit

The following rules apply for claiming the adoption credit:

- The adoption expenses must be for an eligible child. An eligible child is: (a) any child who was under age 18 at the time of the adoption, or (b) a child of any age who is a U.S. citizen or resident alien, and who is physically or mentally incapable of caring for himself or herself.
- You cannot claim this credit if your filing status is MFS.
- To qualify for the credit, your modified AGI must be less than $247,580; phase out begins at $207,580.
- The year you can claim the expenses on your tax return depends on when you paid the expenses, and whether the child was a U.S. citizen or resident at the time the adoption event began. If the child is a U.S.

citizen or resident, you can take the credit whether or not the adoption becomes final.

- You claim the credit by completing Form 8839, Qualified Adoption Expenses, and attaching it to you tax return along with all other adoption-related documents. You must provide the child's name, date of birth, and relevant identifying number (SSN, ITIN, or ATIN).

What if You Received Employer Assistance?

You may be able to exclude from your income, amounts paid to you, or for you, by your employer, under a qualified adoption assistance program, and therefore will not be taxed on these amounts. You may qualify for the income exclusion if you adopted or attempted to adopt a child, and the program paid or reimbursed you for qualified expenses relating to the adoption. The amount of the exclusion is as much as $13,840. You may be able to exclude this amount from your income even if the adoption does not become final.

Employer provided adoption benefits are shown in box 12 of Form W-2 with the code "T". Your exclusion limit is the same as your adoption credit limit. You cannot claim both a credit and exclusion for the same expenses.

The Residential Energy Efficient Property Credit

If you made energy saving improvements to your home by installing an earth-friendly energy source, you may be able to take advantage of the Residential Energy Efficient Property Credit. This tax credit helps individual taxpayers pay for qualified residential alternative energy equipment, such as solar hot water heaters, solar electricity equipment and wind turbines. The credit, which is available through 2018, is valued at 30 percent of the cost of qualified property. There is no cap on the amount of credit available, except for fuel cell property. Generally, you may include labor costs when figuring the credit and you can carry forward any unused portions of this credit to future years. Qualifying equipment must have been installed on or in connection with your home located in the United States.

Home Energy Sources that Qualify for the Energy Efficient Property Credit include the following:

- Geothermal heat pumps.
- Solar water heaters.
- Solar panels.
- Small wind turbines (up to $4,000)
- Fuel cells (up to $500 for each 0.5 kilowatt power capacity, and for primary residence only).

The Credit for the Elderly or the Disabled

If you are at least 65 years old at the end of the tax year, or if you are retired on permanent and total disability, you may be eligible to claim this credit. This credit is a nonrefundable credit. To qualify for the credit, you must be a U.S. citizen or resident for the entire tax year, and must file a joint return if you are married.

You may also be able to claim the credit if you are under 65, but only if:

- You are retired on permanent and total disability.
- You were disabled when you retired.
- You have taxable disability income.
- You did not reach your employer's mandatory retirement age before the tax year began.

You are considered permanently and totally disabled if you cannot engage in any substantial gainful activity because of your physical or mental condition. To be eligible to claim this credit, a physician must certify that you were permanently and totally disabled on the day you retired from work.

To determine if you can claim this credit, you must consider two income limits.

- The amount of your adjusted gross income (AGI).
- The amount of your nontaxable Social Security, annuities, and other nontaxable pensions you receive.

Note that you cannot claim the credit, even if you qualify, if you exceed either of these two income limits, based on your filing status.

The income limits for the various filing statuses are as follows:

- Single, HOH, or QW: - $17,500 AGI or $5,000 Nontaxable Social Security, pension, etc.
- MFJ, and only one spouse qualify: - $20,000 AGI or $5,000 Nontaxable Social Security, pension, etc.
- MFJ, and both spouses qualify: - $25,000 AGI or $7,500 Nontaxable Social Security, pension, etc.
- MFS, and lived apart from spouse all year: - $12,500 AGI or $3,750 Nontaxable Social Security, pension, etc.

You claim this credit by completing Schedule R, Credit for the Elderly or the Disabled, and attaching it to your Form 1040. You can either figure the credit yourself, or you can have the IRS figure it for you.

(Easily available off the shelf tax software will facilitate the completion of the above schedule, and will figure the amount of the credit for inclusion on your tax return.)

-

6 Education Credits, Deductions, and Other Benefits

If you paid eligible higher education expenses during the year for yourself, your spouse, or a dependent on your tax return, you may be able to claim a credit, deduction, or some other benefit on your income tax return. The main objective of this chapter is to make you aware of all the education credits, deductions, and other benefits, which you might be eligible for; to enlighten you how to claim these benefits and to enable you to make an informed decision, based on your particular circumstances, as to which ones would be more beneficial.

The Rules Relating to How to Claim Your Education Credits

Education tax credits can help offset the costs of education. There are basically two types of education credits:

- The American Opportunity Credit. Part of this credit is nonrefundable (60%) and part is refundable (40%).
- The Lifetime Learning Credit, which is a nonrefundable credit.

Any amounts you pay for higher education are reported to you and the IRS on Form 1098-T by the educational institution. To be eligible to claim an education credit, you must have paid qualified expenses for an eligible student to an eligible educational institution. These terms are defined below:

- Qualified expenses are tuition and fees you are required to pay to the educational institution as a condition of enrollment or attendance.
- An eligible student is a student who is enrolled at an eligible educational institution for at least one academic period during the year. An academic period can be a semester, quarter, or summer session.
- An eligible educational institution is any college, university, or vocational school eligible to participate in a student aid program administered by the United States Department of Education.

The following rules apply, concerning claiming an education credit:

- The expenses must be for an academic period that begins in the same year you paid the expenses, or for an academic period that begins in the first three months of the year following the year of payment.

- The expenses can be paid with the proceeds of loans, gifts, or inheritances.
- You cannot claim an education credit if your filing status is MFS.
- The amount of the credit is reduced, and eventually eliminated as your income increases; this phase out depends on your modified adjusted gross income and your filing status.
- You cannot take the credit if you can be claimed as a dependent on another person's tax return.
- You can claim the credit for any qualified expenses paid by a dependent that you claim of your tax return.
- A student, whose exemption is not claimed by the person eligible to claim it, can claim the education credit for qualified expenses on his or her tax return. However, on the student's tax return, he or she is **not** eligible to claim his or her own exemption -- **only** the education credit. (Tax law states that you cannot claim your own exemption if you can be claimed by another person, even though that person might not have claimed you.)

Only **one** person can claim the education credit for a student's expenses in a particular tax year. If you pay higher education costs for a dependent child, either you or the child, but not both, can claim the credit for a particular year. If you claim an exemption for the child, **only** you can claim the credit. Also, any expenses paid by the child are treated as paid by you when figuring the amount of the American opportunity or lifetime learning credit.

The American Opportunity Credit

You can claim this credit for yourself, your spouse, or any dependent that you claim on your tax return.

It is very important to note that the American opportunity credit can be claimed ONLY for the first four years of post-secondary education for each eligible student. This means, then, that this credit is applicable only to college students who are in their freshman, sophomore, junior, and senior years. This credit is therefore not available to post-grad students.

To be eligible to claim the American opportunity credit, the following conditions must be met:

- The student must be enrolled in a program that leads to a degree or other recognized educational credential. This therefore means that the student must be enrolled in an accredited college, university, vocational school, or other accredited postsecondary educational institution.

- The student must be taking at least half the full-time workload for the course of study for at least one academic period during the calendar year.
- The student must not have been convicted of a felony for possessing or distributing a controlled substance.

For purposes of the American opportunity credit, qualified education expenses include the following:

- Tuition and certain related expenses required for enrollment or attendance at the eligible educational institution.
- Expenses for books, supplies, and equipment needed for a course of study, whether or not the materials are purchased from the educational institution. (For example, the expenditure for purchasing a computer could qualify for the credit if the computer is required as a condition of enrollment or attendance at the educational institution.)

The following expenses do not qualify for the credit:

- Room and board.
- Transportation.
- Insurance.
- Medical expenses.
- Student fees, except those that are paid as a condition of enrollment or attendance.
- Expenses paid with non-taxable funds or tax-free educational assistance.
- Any expenses that are used to claim any other tax deduction, credit or educational benefit.

To qualify for the credit, the expenses must be paid for an academic period beginning during the year, or no later than in the first three months of the following year.

The amount of the American opportunity credit is 100% of the first $2,000, plus 25% of the next $2,000 paid for **each** eligible student's qualified tuition and related expenses. Therefore the maximum credit allowed per eligible student is $2,500. The total education credit that you can claim on your tax return, however, will be up to $2,500, multiplied by the number of eligible students that you claim on your tax return. There is therefore no dollar limit per tax return for this credit.

The American opportunity credit is partially a nonrefundable credit, and partially a refundable credit. In essence then, you will be able to reduce your tax liability one dollar for each dollar of the credit for which you are eligible. If the amount of the credit is more than your tax liability, the amount that exceeds your tax liability is refundable to you, up to a maximum of 40 percent of the credit for which you are eligible (that is, up to a maximum of $1,000).

The American opportunity credit is reduced ratably if your modified AGI exceeds $80,000 ($160,000 if filing a joint return). The credit is phased out totally if your modified AGI is greater than $90,000 ($180,000 if filing a joint return).

The Lifetime Learning Credit

You can claim the lifetime learning credit for qualified tuition and related expenses paid for yourself, your spouse, and any dependent on your tax return who is enrolled at any accredited college, university, vocational school, or other accredited postsecondary educational institution. As its name implies, there is no limit for the number of years for which the lifetime learning credit can be claimed for any student.

Unlike the American opportunity credit:

- The lifetime learning credit is not based on the student's workload. It is allowed for one or more courses.
- The lifetime learning credit is not limited to students in the first four years of postsecondary education; therefore expenses for graduate-level degree courses are eligible.
- Felony drug convictions are permitted.
- Expenses for course-related books, supplies, and equipment can be claimed ONLY if they are paid to the institution, as a condition of enrollment or attendance.
- The lifetime learning credit is a nonrefundable credit. This means that it can reduce your tax to zero, but if the credit is more than your tax, the excess credit will not be refunded to you.

To be eligible to claim this credit, your expenses must be for courses taken as part of a postsecondary degree program, or for courses taken to improve or acquire job skills.

The amount of the credit is 20% of the first $10,000 of qualified tuition and related expenses paid for ALL eligible students on your tax return. This means then, that in contrast to the American opportunity credit, there is a dollar limit per tax return for this credit; the maximum amount that can be claimed on any single tax return is $2,000.

To be eligible to claim the lifetime learning credit, your modified AGI must be less than $67,000 ($134,000 if filing jointly). Over this level of earnings, the credit is completely phased out.

How to Claim the Education Credits

You claim both the American opportunity credit and the lifetime learning credit by completing Form 8863, Education Credits (American Opportunity and Lifetime Learning Credits) as follows:

- The American opportunity credit is figured in Part 1.
- The lifetime learning credit is figured in Part II.
- You complete Part III to determine the refundable portion of the American opportunity credit,
- You must include Form 8863 with your tax return.

(Easily available off the shelf tax software will facilitate the completion of Form 8863, and effectively compute the amount of the credit for inclusion on your tax return.)

Other Points to Consider

- In any particular tax year, you can receive only <u>one</u> tax benefit for each student. Therefore, if you choose to claim the American opportunity credit for a student that year, you cannot also claim the lifetime learning credit for that same student.

-
- If you pay qualifying expenses for more than one student, you can choose to take the credits on a per-student, per-year basis. This means that you can claim the American opportunity credit for one student and the lifetime learning credit for another student in the same year, depending on your particular circumstances.

The Student Loan Interest Deduction

You may be able to claim a deduction for any interest that you paid on a qualified student loan. Generally, you can deduct the amount of interest you actually paid, up to a maximum of $2,500. You claim the student loan interest deduction as an adjustment to your income on Schedule 1.

To be eligible for the student loan interest deduction, the following conditions must be met:

- You paid interest on a qualified student loan.
- You are legally obligated to pay interest on a qualified student loan.
- Your filing status is <u>not</u> Married Filing Separately.

- The loan must be for you, your spouse, or a dependent on your tax return at the time you took the loan.
- The loan must be used <u>only</u> for qualified education expenses. Qualified expenses include: tuition, fees, room and board, and any other necessary expenses paid to an eligible educational institution.
- The qualified expenses must be paid within a reasonable period of time before or after you took the loan.
- The loan cannot be from a related person, or made under a qualified employer plan.
- You (and your spouse, if filing jointly) cannot be claimed as a dependent on someone else's tax return.

If you paid interest of $600 or more on a qualified student loan during the year, you should receive a Form 1098-E, Student Loan Interest Statement, from the entity to which you paid the student loan interest.

A qualified student loan is an amount you borrowed to pay for qualified education expenses, at an eligible educational institution, for an eligible student. An eligible educational institution includes most institutions of higher learning.

To be considered an eligible student, you, your spouse, or your dependent must be enrolled in at least half the normal full-time workload in a program leading to a recognized educational credential (graduate or undergraduate).

If you received any nontaxable education benefits, you must reduce your education expenses by these amounts.

A deduction is no longer available if you are unmarried and your adjusted gross income is in the range of $65,000-$80,000. For joint filers, the phase-out is between an adjusted income of $135,000-$165,000. Married individuals filing separately are not eligible for this deduction.

(Easily available off-the-shelf tax software will effectively calculate the deductible portion of your student loan interest, for inclusion in your tax return.)

Tuition and Fees Deduction

You may be able to deduct qualified tuition and related expenses that you pay for yourself, your spouse, or a dependent as a tuition and fees deduction. You can claim up to $4,000 for this deduction.

You cannot take the tuition and fees deduction on your income tax return if your filing status is married filing separately, or if you may be claimed as a dependent on someone else's return. You cannot claim both the tuition and fees deduction and an American opportunity tax credit or lifetime learning credit for the same student in the same tax year. If the educational expenses also qualify as an allowable business expense, then you may be able to claim the tuition and fees deduction in conjunction with a business expense deduction, however you cannot deduct the same expenses twice.

Additionally, you cannot claim a deduction or credit based on expenses paid with tax-free scholarships, fellowships, grants, or education savings account funds, such as a Coverdell education savings account, tax-free savings bond interest, or employer-provided education assistance.

If your modified adjusted gross income exceeds certain limits, your deduction is reduced or eliminated depending on your filing status. You can claim this credit if your modified adjusted gross income is $80,000 or less ($160,000 or less for joint filers). If your modified adjusted gross income is greater than $90,000 ($180,000 for joint filers) cannot claim any of the credit.

The Coverdell Education Savings Account (ESA)

A Coverdell Education Savings Account (ESA) is an account created as an incentive to help parents and students save for education expenses. It is a trust or custodial account created in the U.S. for the purpose of paying the qualified higher education expenses of the beneficiary (child) under the age of 18. The contribution is limited to $2,000 for each beneficiary; it is not tax deductible, but amounts deposited in the account can grow tax-free until distributed.

If distributions from a Coverdell ESA exceed qualified education expenses, the excess distribution will be taxable to the beneficiary, and will usually be subject to an additional 10% tax. There are some exceptions to the 10% addition tax rule, which include the death or disability of the beneficiary, or if the beneficiary receives a qualified scholarship.

Qualified education expenses include tuition, books, supplies, and room and board. There are contribution limits to a Coverdell ESA based on your modified AGI. Your allowable contribution to an ESA is gradually reduced and phased out if your modified AGI is between $95,000 and $110,000 (between $190,000 and $220,000 if filing MFJ).

The following requirements must be met in creating a Coverdell ESA:

- The trustee or custodian must be a bank in the U.S. approved by the IRS.

- The custodian can only accept a contribution if: (a) it is in cash, (b) is made before the beneficiary reaches age 18, or for a special needs beneficiary over 18, and (c) is made by the due date of the contributor's tax return, excluding extensions.
- Money in the account cannot be invested in life insurance contracts.
- Money in the account cannot be combined with other property, except in a common trust fund or common investment fund.
- If there is a balance in the Coverdell ESA when the beneficiary reaches age 30, it must generally be distributed within 30 days. The portion representing earnings on the account will be taxable, and will also be subject to the additional 10% tax. The beneficiary may avoid these taxes, however, by rolling over the full balance into another Coverdell ESA for another family member.
- The balance in a Coverdell ESA account must be withdrawn within 30 days after the earlier of the following two events: (a) the date the beneficiary reaches age 30, unless the beneficiary is a special needs beneficiary, or (b) the beneficiary's death.

The Qualified Tuition Program (529 Plan)

A qualified tuition program, also known as a 529 plan or program, is a tax-advantaged savings plan designed to encourage saving for future college costs. 529 plans, legally known as "qualified tuition plans," are sponsored by states, state agencies, or educational institutions, and are authorized by Section 529 of the Internal Revenue Code. Although contributions are not tax-deductible on your federal tax return, a 529 plan is a program set up to allow you to prepay, or contribute to an account established for paying a student's qualified education expenses at an eligible educational institution.

Previously, elementary and secondary school expenses were not considered qualified education expenses. The TCJA, however, has broadened the definition of qualified education expenses by authorizing an annual qualified distribution of contributions made after 12/31/17 of up to $10,000 from a taxpayer's 529 plans for elementary and secondary school tuition..

The following rules apply to 529 plans:

- The designated beneficiary: This is generally the student (or future student) for whom the qualified tuition program is intended to provide benefits. You can change the designated beneficiary after participation in the program begins.
- Contributions: Your contributions to a qualified tuition program on behalf of any beneficiary cannot be more than the amount necessary to

provide for the qualified education expenses of the beneficiary. There are no income restrictions on the individual contributors.

- Distributions: The part of the distribution representing the amounts paid or contributed to a qualified tuition program are not included in taxable income; they are a return of the investment in the plan. The designated beneficiary does not have to include in taxable income any earnings distributed from a qualified tuition program if the total distribution is less than or equal to the qualified education expenses.
- Qualified educational expenses: These expenses are the tuition, fees, books, supplies, and equipment required for enrollment or attendance at an eligible educational institution. They also include the reasonable costs of room and board for a designated beneficiary who is at least a half-time student.
- Coordination with American opportunity and lifetime learning credit: An American opportunity or lifetime learning credit can be claimed in the same year the beneficiary takes a tax-free distribution from a qualified tuition program, as long as the same expenses are not used for both benefits. This means that after the beneficiary reduces qualified education expenses by the tax-free assistance, he or she must further reduce them by the expenses taken into account in determining the credit.
- Coordination with Coverdell ESA distributions: If a designated beneficiary receives distributions from both a qualified tuition program and a Coverdell ESA in the same year, and the total of these distributions is more than the beneficiary's adjusted higher education expenses, the expenses must be allocated between the distributions. For purposes of this allocation, you must disregard any qualified elementary and secondary education expenses.
- Additional tax on taxable distributions: Generally, if you receive a taxable distribution, you must pay a 10% additional tax on the amount that you have to include in income.

Some states will allow you to deduct contributions to your 529 plan on your state tax return, and some might require that the contribution be made to that state's plan for it to be deductible. Not all states have this requirement, so you should check with your state's tax department or website, to see what your state's position is.

The Education Savings Bond Program

You may exclude from taxable income all or part of the interest received on the redemption of qualified U.S. Savings Bond (Series EE bonds issued after 1989) if the proceeds are used for higher educational expenses during the

same year. The expenses must be for tuition and fees only, and can be for you, your spouse, or your dependents.
If the higher educational expenses are more than or equal to the proceeds (interest and principal) from the bonds, you exclude all the interest.

If the educational expenses are less than the proceeds, only part of the interest can be excluded from income. To figure the excludable amount, apply the following formula: Excludable interest = interest x (educational expenses divided by bond proceeds).

To be eligible to exclude interest, your modified adjusted gross income must be less than $94,550 ($149,300 if filing MFJ or QW).

6 Reporting Your Income

This chapter looks at the various types of income that are generally reported on your tax return. Income that you receive during the year can be either earned or unearned, taxable or nontaxable, depending on your particular circumstances, and must be properly reported on your tax return in accordance with tax law.

Defining Taxable and Non-taxable Income

Income you receive can be in the form of money, goods, services, or property. Establishing what falls under taxable income or non-taxable income can be a little bit confusing for some people. Although most income received is taxable, there are certain types of income, which are not. Taxable income comprises all income you receive during the tax year that tax law does not specifically exempt from income tax. All such income is subject to income tax, regardless of whether the income was received in the form of cash or in the form of non-cash property.

Taxable Income

Typically, taxable income will comprise the following:

- Wages, salaries, tips, and other employee compensation.
- Income from self-employment.
- Taxable interest.
- Ordinary and qualified dividends.
- Taxable refunds of state and local income taxes (in some cases).
- Capital and other gains.
- IRA distributions.
- Pensions and annuities.
- Income from real estate rental.
- Income from royalties.
- Income from partnerships, S corporations, and trusts.
- Income from farming.
- Unemployment compensation.
- Some Social Security benefits.
- Canceled debt.
- Some income from court award and damages (see below).
- Income from all other sources that are not tax exempt.

Income is taxable when it is constructively received. Income is constructively received when it is made available to you without restrictions, even though it does not necessarily have to be in your possession. Examples of situations in which income is constructively received include the following:

- Interest credited to your bank account, regardless of when the funds are withdrawn.
- Debts that are forgiven or paid by someone else (if it was not a gift or loan).
- Payments received by your agent on your behalf.
- A check received or made available to you.
- Wages that are garnished. These are treated as been constructively received by you.
- Income you receive in advance, such as rents, interest, and pay for services to be performed later.

Nontaxable Income

Nontaxable or tax exempt income is income that is not subject to income tax, and you do not report these on your tax return. Nontaxable income includes the following:

- Child support.
- Alimony
- Federal tax refunds.
- Interest on state or local government obligations, such as municipal bonds.
- Welfare and other public assistance benefits.
- Workers' compensation and similar payments for sickness and injury.
- Meals and lodgings provided by your employer. These will be excluded from your taxable income if: (a) the meals are furnished on your employer's business premises, (b) the meals are furnished for the convenience of your employer, and (c) the lodging is required for employment.
- Employee achievements awards.
- Employer contributions to a medical savings account.
- Most life insurance proceeds received by beneficiaries upon death of the policyholder.
- Accident and health insurance proceeds.
- Casualty insurance.
- Education assistance program. Your employer must exclude from your taxable income, the first $5,250 of any qualified educational assistance paid to you each year. The payments do not have to be for work-related courses and can be for both undergraduate and graduate-level courses. Educational assistance includes payments for: tuition, fees and similar

payments, books, supplies, and equipment. Educational assistance does not include expenses for meals, lodging, and transportation.

- Part or all of Social Security benefits.
- Part of scholarships and fellowship grants. Only a candidate for a degree program can exclude from income amounts received as a qualified scholarship. The amounts excluded must be for tuition and fees, books, supplies, and equipment required for courses. Any amounts received for room and board are taxable.
- Housing allowances for members of the clergy.
- Veterans' disability benefits. Allowances paid by the department of Veterans Affairs are not included in taxable income.
- Military allowances.
- Gifts, bequests, inheritances (these may be subject to other taxes, such as gift tax).
- Disaster relief grants.
- Damages for physical injury or sickness.

Earned Income

There are two ways to have earned income: (a) you work for someone who pays you, or (b) you work in a business you own. Earned income therefore, essentially comprises:

- Wages, salaries, tips and other employee compensation earned from performing personal services.
- Net earnings from self-employment, or from operating a trade or business.

In this section, we shall proceed to look at earned income received in the form of salaries, wages, tips, and other employee compensation. We shall look at self-employment income in a subsequent section.

Salaries and Wages

Salaries and wages are basically the most common type of earned income reported on most tax returns, and include the following:

- Salaries and wages received as compensation from your employer for work or services that you provide.
- Other compensation received from your employer in the form of awards, bonuses, sick pay, severance pay, employer-provided car for personal use, and other taxable employee benefits.
- Compensation received in the form of goods, services, and property; these are also taxable income.

- All other income received from your employer that is not specifically excluded by law from taxation. These are taxable and must be reported.

Form W-2 Wage and Tax Statement

The Form W-2, Wage and Tax Statement is the form used to report wages paid to employees, and also, the taxes withheld from those wages. Employers are required to complete a Form W-2 for each employee to whom they pay a salary, wage, or other compensation as part of the employment relationship. Form W-2 is reported to both you and the IRS, and your employer must mail out your Form W-2 to you by January 31.

You must report your Form W-2 information on your tax return as follows:

- Box 1 of Form W-2 reports total wages, tips, and other compensation. This is your gross pay before federal and state taxes, Social Security, and Medicare taxes are taken out.
- If the information in box 1 of your W-2 is incorrect, you must contact your employer immediately, who must issue Form W-2c, correcting the error.
- If you received more than one W-2, because you had more than one employer during the year, the amounts in box 1 of all your W-2s must be added together, and entered on your tax return.
- Even if, for whatever reason, you did not receive a Form W-2 from your employer, you must still report your income on your tax return.

Wages and Compensation Reported in Box 1 of Form W-2

All wages and compensation reported in box 1 of your Form W-2 must be entered on your tax return. The categories of income reported in box 1 include the following:

- Regular pay.
- Advance commissions.
- Back pay awards.
- Sick pay.
- Holiday gifts.
- Severance pay.
- Travel and other business expense reimbursements (in some cases).
- Employer provided vehicles.
- Supplemental unemployment benefits.
- Employer contributions to a non-qualified retirement plan.
- Disability income from an employer-paid plan.

Income from Tips

Tips are amounts that you receive from customers if you work for certain food and drink establishments that serve customers, for example, a restaurant. All tips received are taxable income, therefore all cash and non-cash tips that you receive from customers must be reported as taxable income on your tax return. You must keep a daily record of all tips received so that you can: (a) report tips to your employer, (b) report tips accurately on your tax return, and (c) prove tips; should the IRS question your return.

Reporting Tips to Your Employer

Tax law requires that you report to your employer all cash, checks, or credit card tips of $20 or more received for any month from any one job. You report your tip income on Form 4070, Employee's Report of Tips to Employer, or on a similar statement. This report is due on the 10th day of the month after the month the tips are received. This statement must be signed by the employee and must show the following details: (a) your name, address, and SSN, (b) the month or period the report covers, and (c) the total tips received.

The rules relating to the reporting of tips are as follows:

- Reported tips are included in the amount shown in box 1 of Form W-2.
- Your employer must withhold Social Security and Medicare taxes from your tips.
- Any Social Security and Medicare taxes that were not withheld by your employer for tips must be reported as additional tax on your return.
- You are not required to report the value of non-cash tips to your employer (but see below).
- If you do not report your tips of $20 or more, as is required by tax law, you may be subject to a penalty.

How to Account for Tips Received of Under $20

You are not required to report tips received of under $20 a month to your employer, because these tips are not subject to Social Security or Medicare taxes. These tips, however, are subject to income tax, and must be reported on your tax return. You must total all your tips received under $20, and add these to the value of any non-cash tips you might have received. This total must then be added to your wages in box 1 of your W-2, and reported on your tax return.

Unreported Tips of Over $20

If you did not report your tips of $20 or more per month to your employer, you must also add these tips to the amount entered on your tax return. You must now use Form 4137, Social Security and Medicare Tax on Unreported Tip Income, to figure and report your Social Security and Medicare taxes on these tips, and report them as additional taxes on your tax return.

How to Report Allocated Tips

Allocated tips are tips that are assigned to you by your employer in addition to the tips you report, and are reported to you in box 8 of your Form W-2. Tip allocation is only required if you work for certain food and drink establishments and your reported tips are less than your share of a required percentage of food and drink sales.

You must report your allocated tips as follows:

- If allocated tips are shown in box 8 of your Form W-2, that amount must be included in your gross income unless you have proof of actual tips, in which case you would report your actual tips.
- You must include allocated tips in your gross income by adding them to the amount shown in box 1 of Form W-2 and entering the total on your tax return. You must now use Form 4137 to figure and report the Social Security and Medicare taxes you owe on these allocated tips.

Definition of Statutory Employees

Statutory employees are treated as independent contractors under the common law rules, but they are treated as employees by statute for certain employment tax purposes. You are a statutory employee if you fall within one of the four categories below:

- A driver who distributes beverages (other than milk), meat, vegetables, fruit, or bakery products; or who picks up and delivers laundry or dry cleaning, if the driver is an agent, or is working on commission.
- A full-time life insurance sales agent whose principal business activity is selling life insurance or annuity contracts primarily for one insurance company.
- An individual who works at home on materials supplied by his or her employer that must be returned to the employer, who also furnishes the specifications for the work to be done.
- A full-time traveling or city salesperson who works on behalf of his or her employer and turns in orders to his or her employer from wholesalers, retailers, contractors, or operators of hotels, restaurants,

or other similar establishments. The work performed for the employer must be the salesperson's principal business activity.

If you are a statutory employee, your employer is required to withhold Social Security and Medicare taxes (but not income tax) from your wages, if all three of the following conditions apply:

- The service contract states or implies that substantially all the services are to be performed personally by the employee.
- The employee does not have a substantial investment in the equipment and property used to perform the services (other than an investment in transportation facilities).
- The services are performed on a continuous basis for the same employer.

If you are a Statutory Employee, your employer will check box 13 on your Form W-2. In this case, you will report your income using one of the following 2 methods:

- If you incurred no expenses in earning the income being reported, you must enter the amount in box 1 of your Form W-2 on your tax return
- If you incurred expenses in earning the income, then you must complete a Schedule C or C-EZ, on which you will enter the income and related expenses, and report the net income your tax return.

What If You Do Not Receive a Form W-2 from Your Employer?

The IRS requires that employers should send out all Forms W-2 by January 31. The IRS also requires that tax returns should only be prepared based on information on a Form W-2. Therefore, tax returns should not be prepared from pay stubs. However, if you are unable to obtain your Form W-2 from your employer by February 15, you can file your tax return with a Form 4852, Substitute for Form W-2, Wage and Tax Statement. In this case, you will have to swear under penalties of perjury that you have been unable to obtain your Form W-2, and have indeed made all reasonable efforts to obtain your Form W-2 from your employer. In this case, a last pay stub may be used to complete Form 4852. You must attach Form 4852 to the return, estimating income and withholding taxes as accurately as possible. If you receive your W-2 subsequent to filing your return with Form 4852, and the information it contains does not match the income or withholding reported on the return, you must file an amended return to correct the situation. The IRS will not accept Form 4852 before February 15.

Other Income Not Reported On Form W-2

There are some other types of employer related incomes that are not reported on a Form W-2, but which must be included in gross income on your tax return. These types of income include the following:

- The taxable portion of scholarships and fellowships that you receive.
- Wages received as a household employee, if less than $1700.
- The amount of any dependent care benefits that cannot be excluded from income by tax law.
- Any employer provided adoption or moving expense reimbursements, which by tax law cannot be excluded from income.

How to Report Income Received On Form 1099-MISC

If you are a self-employed contractor, the income you receive from your employer will be reported to you on a Form 1099-MISC instead of on a Form W-2. Your income from self-employment will be reported in box 7 of Form 1099- MISC. You must report the amount in box 7 of your Form 1099-MISC on a Schedule C or C-EZ (see business section), from which you can deduct all related expenses incurred in earning the income. You then report the net amount on your tax return.

Nontaxable Employee Compensation (Fringe Benefits)

Many fringe benefits you receive from your employer are either tax-free or tax-deferred, and are specifically excluded from your taxable income by tax law. Therefore, you should never include a tax-free fringe benefit in your gross income, because you are not required to pay tax on it. Tax-free fringe benefits include the following:

- Health care benefits, and the cost of group life insurance coverage of up to $50,000.
- Cafeteria plans.
- Dependent care assistance of up to $5,000.
- Adoption assistance of up to $13,840.
- Stock options.

A tax-deferred fringe benefit is not included in your gross income in the year you receive it, and so, it is not taxed until later years. A tax-deferred fringe benefit typically includes your employer's contribution to a qualified retirement plan, and also your contributions to a retirement plan under a qualified deferred compensation plan set up by your employer, such as a

401(k) plan. With a qualified deferred compensation plan, the following must be noted:

- Your contributions to such a plan is shown in box 12 of Form W-2, with the code letter D.
- You pay Social Security and Medicare taxes on the deferred compensation in the year you receive it, but not income tax.
- Social Security and Medicare wages shown in box 3 and 5 of your Form W-2 will be different from the amount of wages shown in box 1.
- Retirement plan distributions are taxed in the year when you withdraw the funds from your retirement plan.

Certain other fringe benefits are specifically exempt from tax. These include the following:

- No-additional-cost service: This is where your employer provides you with a service offered for sale to customers, and does not incur substantial additional cost in providing you with the service.
- Qualified employee discount: This is where your employer allows you to buy property or service at a discount and the discount is not more than the profit percentage, or is not more than 20% of the price offered to customers.
- De minimis (minimal) fringe benefit: This is a fringe benefit so small in value that it would be impractical for your employer to account for it (e.g., personal use of your employer's copying machine, tickets to theatre or sporting events, turkey at Thanksgiving, etc.)
- Athletic facilities: Your employer should exclude from your income the value of an on-premises athletic facility, as long as it is not made available to the general public, and substantially all its use is by employees, their spouses, and their dependent children.
- Achievement awards: Your employer should exclude from your income the value of achievement awards up to $1,600 ($400 for awards that are not "qualified plan awards").

How to Report Your Withholdings

Income tax is essentially a pay as you earn tax. You are generally expected to pay at least 90% of your expected tax liability during the tax year as you earn the income. As an employee, you generally meet this obligation by having taxes withheld from your salary. Tax may also be withheld from other types of income, and for each type of income from which tax is withheld, the payer reports to you and the IRS on a different form.

Tax law mandates that your employer must withhold income taxes from your wages, but you can claim an exemption from withholding if you expect to have no tax liability. You determined how much tax you want withheld from your wages by completing Form W-4, Employee's Withholding Allowance Certificate. Your employer will base your withholding on the amount you earn, and on the information you provide on Form W-4.

On Form W-4 you provide two basic types of information:

- Whether your employer is to withhold tax at the single or at the married rate.
- You can also advise your employer whether you want an additional amount withheld.

You need to be aware that an incorrectly completed Form W-4 can result in either too little, or too much tax being withheld.

Your Federal withholding is reported in box 2 of Form W-2. You must enter the total box 2 amounts of all your Form W-2s on you tax return.

How to Report Clergy Income

Members of the clergy are in many ways treated like other taxpayers, but there are special tax treatments that recognize their position as employees of a church. For tax purposes, members of the clergy may be treated as either employees or independent contractors.
It is very important to note that members of the clergy are always considered self-employed for the purposes of Social Security and Medicare taxes.
Generally, you are an employee if the church or organization has the legal right to control both what you do and how you do it, even if you have considerable discretion and freedom of action.

If you are employed by a congregation for a salary, you are generally a common-law employee, and income from the exercise of your ministry is considered wages for income tax purposes. However, amounts received directly from members of the congregation, such as fees for performing marriages, baptisms, or other personal services, are considered self-employment income.

In either case, with approval from the IRS, members of the clergy have an opportunity to bow out of the Social Security system and not pay this tax. To request an exemption from self-employment tax, you must file Form 4361, Application for Exemption From Self-Employment Tax for Use by Ministers, Members of Religious Orders and Christian Science Practitioners, with the IRS. This exemption stops the requirement for paying self-employment tax, but it will also prevent you from receiving benefits during the period of exemption.

83

If you are treated as an employee:

- You will receive a Form W-2 statement of income from your employer (church) organization.
- Your employer, however, should not withhold Social Security tax, because a minister is always considered self-employed when it comes to Social Security.
- Your federal income tax withholding is voluntary, but if income tax is not withheld, you must make quarterly estimated tax payments.
- Your housing allowance is generally exempt from income tax as long as it is spent for housing related expenses.

If you are treated as an independent contractor:

- You will receive a Form 1099 MISC from the organizations receiving your services.
- You must file a self-employed tax return using Schedule C or C-EZ.
- There will be no withholdings for Social Security and federal income tax.
- Any housing allowance received is not included in income.

Even though, for Social Security tax and Medicare tax purposes, you are considered a self-employed individual in performing your ministerial services, you may be considered an employee for income tax or retirement plan purposes. For income tax or retirement plan purposes, some of your income may be considered self-employment income and other income may be considered wages.

If you are a minister performing ministerial services, you must include in income, offerings and fees received for marriages, baptisms, funerals, etc., in addition to salary. If the offering is made to the religious institution, however, it is not taxable.

Since members of the clergy are considered self-employed for the purposes of Social Security and Medicare taxes, the church does not withhold Social Security and Medicare taxes from a pastor's salary the way it does for lay employees. Likewise, the church does not have to pay the employer's share of Social Security and Medicare taxes for the pastor as it does for lay employees. Clergy are not subject to mandatory federal tax withholding, however, the pastor may elect to voluntarily have the church withhold these taxes in lieu of filing quarterly personal estimated taxes. Pastors are required to file Schedule SE with their tax return. This form is used to calculate the pastor's self-employment taxes for Social Security and Medicare.

A minister's housing allowance, sometimes called a parsonage allowance or a rental allowance, is excludable from gross income for income tax purposes, but not for self-employment tax purposes. The Housing Exclusion Allowance amounts, however, are subject to Social Security and Medicare taxes, and must be added to taxable salary by the pastor, for calculating taxes due on Schedule SE.

If you own your home, however, you may still claim deductions for mortgage interest and real property taxes. If your housing allowance exceeds the lesser of your reasonable salary, the fair rental value of the home, or your actual expenses, you must include the amount of the excess as other income.

Note, then, that the fair rental value of a parsonage or the housing allowance is excludable from income only for income tax purposes. No exclusion applies for self-employment tax purposes. For Social Security and Medicare tax purposes, a duly ordained, licensed or commissioned minister is considered self-employed, therefore you will pay SE tax on both your wages and self-employment income. This means that your salary on Form W-2, the net profit on Schedule C or C-EZ, and your housing allowance, less any employee business expenses, are subject to self-employment tax on Schedule SE.

The Foreign Earned Income Exclusion

For tax year 2018, you can be eligible to exclude up to $104,100 of foreign earned income, foreign housing exclusion, or the foreign housing deduction, if all three of the following requirements are satisfied:

- Your tax home must be in a foreign country.
- You must have foreign earned income.
- You must be either: (a) a U.S. citizen who is a bona fide resident of a foreign country for at least an entire year, (b) a U.S. resident alien who is a citizen or national of a country with which the United States as an income tax treaty in effect, and you were a resident of that country for at least an entire year, or (c) a U.S. citizen or a U.S. resident alien who is physically in a foreign country for at least 330 full days during any period of 12 consecutive months.

Foreign earned income is defined as pay received for personal services performed, such as wages, salaries, or professional fees.

Definition of Unearned Income

Unearned income is any income you receive from sources other than wages, salaries, tips, other employee compensation, or from self-employment. Unearned income includes the following:

- Interest and dividends.
- Pensions.
- Social Security benefits.
- Unemployment benefits.
- State and local tax refunds.
- Income from court award and damages.
- Cancellation of debt.

Interest Income

Interest is income earned through depositing money in savings programs, from buying certificate of deposits (CDs) or bonds, or from lending money. It includes interest receive from your bank accounts, interest you receive on loans you make to others, and interest from most other sources.

Interest that you receive or which is credited to your account and can be withdrawn; is taxable income in the year it becomes available to you.

Interest earned over $10 must be reported to you on a Form 1099-INT by the financial institution from which the interest was earned. The interest is reported to you in box 3 of Form 1099-INT.

The following rules relate to reporting interest income on your tax return:

- If you received interest of over $1,500, this must be reported on Part 1 of Schedule B, Interest and Ordinary Dividends.
- If you have invested in CDs, which will mature after more than one year, you must include part of the interest as income for each year.
- If you suffered an early withdrawal penalty for withdrawing money from CDs or other time-deposit savings account before maturity, that penalty is reported to you in box 2 of Form 1099-INT. You can deduct this penalty as an adjustment to income on your tax return.
- If you received interest from partnerships or S corporations, this is taxable interest. This interest is reported to you on a Schedule K-1.
- If you received interest on the proceeds of a life insurance policy, this interest is taxable, although the proceeds paid from the policy is generally not taxable.
- Interest you receive on tax refunds is taxable income.

- If you receive a gift for opening a bank account with a savings institution, the fair market value of the gift must be reported as interest in the year you received it.
- You must report your taxable interest on line 2a of Form 1040. You report tax-exempt interest on line 2b, and this is not included as a part of your gross income.

Dividend Income

Dividends are distributions that you receive from corporations, and can be in the form of money, stock, or other property paid to you by a corporation. Any dividends you receive over $10 must be reported to you by your broker on a Form 1099-DIV. You may also receive dividends from a partnership, estate, trust, or an S corporation. Dividends from these sources are reported to you on a Schedule K-1.
If you receive total dividends of over $1,500, this must be reported on Part II of Schedule B.

The following are the main types of dividends you might receive:

- Ordinary dividends: These are paid out of the profits of corporations, and are taxable income.
- Qualified dividends: These are ordinary dividends, which are taxed as capital gains. Qualified dividends are taxed at a maximum rate of 20% (0% for those people who are in a tax bracket of lower than 25%, and 15% for those within the 25% to 35% tax bracket).
- Capital gain distributions: Mutual funds pass capital gains to investors as capital gain distributions, and these amounts are taxed as capital gains. They are reported to you in box 2a of Form 1099-DIV, and you must report them directly on your tax return.
- Non-dividend distributions: These represent a return of capital, and are not taxable unless the amount you receive exceeds the amount you originally invested, in which case, the excess would be reported as a capital gain.
- Credit union dividends: A "dividend" received from a credit union is actually interest, and must be reported on either Part 1 Schedule B, or directly on your tax return.
- Dividend reinvestment: If you are involved in a dividend reinvestment plan, (where the institution allows you to use dividends to purchase additional shares instead of receiving the dividends in cash), you must report the dividends reinvested as income.

State or Local Income Tax Refunds

These tax refunds are reported to you on a Form 1099-G, Certain Government Payments, and can either be taxable or nontaxable, depending on your particular circumstances.

- Your state or local tax refund may be fully or partially taxable if you itemized deductions in the previous year, and claimed your state and local income tax withholdings as an itemized deduction. To determine the amount of your state or local tax refund that may be taxable, the appropriate worksheet must be completed. You report your taxable refund as income on your tax return.
- If you took the standard deduction, however, or claimed the state and local general sales taxes instead of income tax, as your itemized deduction, then the state or local tax refund is not taxable.

Unemployment Compensation

Any unemployment compensation received is fully taxable. If you received unemployment compensation, it is reported to you on a Form 1099-G, and you must report it as income.

Income from Court Awards and Damages

The following settlement amounts received by compromise or judgment must be included in taxable income:

- Interest on any award.
- Compensation for lost wages or lost profits.
- Punitive damages.
- Amounts received in settlement of pension rights (if you did not contribute to the plan).
- Damages for patent or copyright infringement, for breach of contract, or for interference with business operations.
- Back pay and damages for emotional distress received to satisfy a claim under the Civil Rights Act of 1964.
- Attorney fees and court costs where the underlying recovery is included in income.

You must report these items of income as Other Income on Schedule 1, line 21. Note, however, that any amounts received as damages to compensate for a physical injury or physical illness, are not taxable, and should not be included in taxable income.

Cancellation of Debt

A cancellation of a debt will result in taxable income. The logic is that when you borrowed the money you were not required to include the loan proceeds in your taxable income, because you had an obligation to repay the lender. When that obligation is subsequently forgiven, the amount you received as loan proceeds must now be reported as taxable income, because you no longer have an obligation to repay the lender. The forgiven amount must be reported to you and the IRS on a Form 1099-C, Cancellation of Debt. You report a cancellation of debt as Other Income on Schedule 1, line 21.

Note, however, that a cancellation of debt is not general taxable in the case of non-recourse loans. A non-recourse loan is a loan for which the lender's only remedy in case of default is to repossess the property being financed or used as collateral. The lender, therefore, cannot pursue you personally in case of default. Forgiveness of a non-recourse loan resulting from a foreclosure, therefore, generally does not result in cancellation of debt income.

Reporting Gambling Winning

Gambling winnings are taxable income, and if the conditions below exist, they must be reported to you on Form W-2G, Certain Gambling Winnings:

- The winnings (not reduced by the wager) are $1,200 or more from a bingo game or slot machine.
- The winnings (reduced by the wager) are $1,500 or more from a keno game.
- The winnings (reduced by the wager or buy-in) are more than $5,000 from a poker tournament.
- The winnings (except winnings from bingo, slot machines, keno, and poker tournaments) reduced by the wager at the option of the payer, are: (a) $600 or more, and (b) at least 300 times the amount of the wager.
- The winnings are subject to federal income tax withholding (either regular gambling withholding or backup withholding).

Gambling winnings fall into the category of Miscellaneous Income, and you must report your gambling winnings as Other Income. Gambling income also includes winnings from lotteries, raffles, horse and dog races, casino winnings, as well as the fair market value of prizes won, such as cars, houses, trips, and all other non-cash prizes.

While gambling winnings are taxed, you may find some relief from taxation by deducting losses. You may, however, only deduct your losses from gambling if you itemize deductions, and you may deduct losses only up to the amount of your winnings, so that they cancel each other out at the best. You may not deduct more than the amount of your winnings.

If you are a professional gambler, then your gambling activity is treated as a business, and you report your winnings and all your losses on Schedule C.

All Other Income

Any other types of income must be reported on your tax return on Schedule 1, line 21. Such other income includes the following:

- Prizes and awards.
- Hobby income.
- Compensation for jury duty.
- Distributions from a Coverdell education savings account or from a Qualified Tuition Program (529 Plan).
- Distribution from a Health Savings Account or an Archer Medical savings account.
- Alaska Permanent Fund dividends.
- Reimbursements or recoveries of amounts that were claimed as a tax deduction or credit in a previous year.
- Dividends received on a life insurance policy.
- Income from bribes.
- Fair market value of property found.
- Kickbacks, side commissions, push money, etc.
- Rewards.
- Stolen money or property, unless, in the same year, it was returned it to its lawful owner

Other Points to Consider

- Interest earned on U.S. obligations such as Treasury bills, notes, and bonds, is subject to federal tax but is exempt from all state and local taxes, so you should be careful not to include these amounts in your state and local tax returns.

-
- Interest received on the redemption of qualified U.S. savings bonds is tax exempt if it is used to pay for higher educational expenses during the same year.

- Interest received from municipal bonds is exempt from federal tax, so you should not report these amounts as income on your tax return.

- If you are a U.S. citizen, and you receive interest and dividends from sources outside of the United States, these amounts are taxable income, unless exempt by tax law, and you must report these amounts on your tax return. This holds true whether you live outside the U.S., and whether you receive a Form 1099-INT from the payer.

- Stock dividends, that is, dividends paid in the form of stock splits; these reduce your basis in stock, and are not taxable income.

- Dividends you receive from life insurance are not taxable until the amount of dividends you receive exceed the total premiums you pay.

- You can exclude from income any interest credited on frozen deposits that could not be withdrawn because the financial institution was either bankrupt or insolvent.

- U.S. payers of income other than wages, such as dividends and royalties are required to withhold tax at a flat rate of 30% on non-wage income paid to nonresident aliens.

7 Adjustments to Income

Adjustments to income are sometimes referred to as "above the line" deductions. These adjustments are comprised of certain expenses, which the IRS allows you to use to directly reduce your gross income, and which in essence, are really tax deductions. You do not need to itemize deductions on Schedule A, in order to claim these expenses, instead, you enter them on Schedule 1, lines 23 to 33. The objective of this chapter is to make you aware of the all these adjustments, some of which are oftentimes overlooked, which you can take directly against your gross income, and thus reduce your AGI, and ultimately, your tax liability.

Your total adjustments to income are subtracted from your total income to figure adjusted gross income or AGI. Your AGI is the baseline for figuring out what you will owe to the IRS, or what will be refunded to you. There are several adjustments (deductions), which you may be eligible to deduct, and we shall explore these deductions below.

Educator Expense Deduction

If you are an eligible educator, you can deduct up to $250 ($500 if married filing jointly and both spouses are educators, but not more than $250 each) of any unreimbursed expenses. Qualified expenses are amounts you paid or incurred for books, supplies, computer equipment (including related software and services), other equipment, and supplementary materials that you use in the classroom. You claim this deduction on Schedule 1, line 23.

You are an eligible educator if:

- You are a teacher, instructor, counselor, principal, or aide for kindergarten through grade 12.

AND

- You work at least 900 hours a school year in a school that provides elementary or secondary education as determined under state law.

The IRA Deduction

If you contribute to a traditional IRA, you may be able to deduct some or all of your contributions. You deduct your IRA contribution on schedule 1, line 32. Investing in an IRA can be an excellent and very flexible tax-planning tool, because you can reduce your taxable income by contributing money to a traditional IRA, and contributions can be made as late as the first due date for filing your tax return, which is normally April 15 of the following year. The rules concerning the deductibility of your IRA contributions are as follows:

- Generally, you can deduct contributions made to a traditional IRA.
- Contributions are tax-deferred when made, but amounts are taxed when you eventually begin to withdraw them from the IRA.
- You claim your IRA deduction directly on your tax return.
- You cannot deduct contributions you make to a Roth IRA.

The amount that you are allowed to deduct for your IRA investment is generally the same as the amount you contribute. The IRS, however, limits the amount that you can contribute to an IRA each year.

Your contribution to an IRA cannot exceed the **lesser** of the following amounts:

- $5,500 ($6,500 if age 50 and over).
- Your total taxable compensation for the year. (Taxable compensation comprises your earned income plus alimony or separate maintenance payments received.)
-

If you (or your spouse) are covered by an employer retirement plan, the deductible amount is reduced or eliminated, depending on your filing status and modified adjusted gross income. If you are covered by such a plan, your employer should check the retirement plan box; that is, box 13 of your W-2.

(Easily available off-the-shelf tax software will effectively complete the worksheet, and compute how much of your contribution is deductible, for inclusion on your tax return.)

If the amount of your IRA deduction has been reduced or has been eliminated, by virtue of your income, you can still contribute the full permitted amount to your IRA, even though you won't be able to claim a deduction.

In this situation, the following rules apply:

- You should report on Form 8606, any part of the contribution you made to an IRA that you were not able to deduct as an adjustment to income.
- If you do not report your nondeductible contributions on Form 8606, this could be to your detriment, because you will be taxed again on these contributions when you withdraw them from the fund.
- If you and your spouse both have nondeductible contributions, you must both file a separate Form 8606.
- You must file Form 8606 even if you are not required to file a tax return.
- If you do not file Form 8606 when required, you may be slapped with a fine of $50.

The Student Loan Interest Deduction

You may be able to deduct interest you pay on a qualified student loan. This deduction can be up to a maximum of $2,500 of qualified student loan interest paid each year. You deduct qualified student loan interest on Schedule 1, line 33.

The rules for deducting student loan interest are as follows:

- You must have paid interest on a qualified student loan.
- You are legally obligated to pay interest on a qualified student loan.
- Your cannot claim a student loan deduction if your filing status is MFS.
- Your modified adjusted gross income must less than a specified amount which is set annually.
- You and your spouse, if filing jointly, cannot be claimed as dependents on someone else's return.
- The deduction begins to phase out at $130,000 if filing MFJ, and is completely phased out for income over $160,000. ($65,000 to $80,000 for any other filing status).

Tuition and Fees Deduction

You may be able to deduct qualified tuition and related expenses that you pay for yourself, your spouse, or a dependent as a tuition and fees deduction. You can claim up to $4,000 for this deduction. You claim this deduction on Schedule 1.

You cannot take the tuition and fees deduction on your income tax return if your filing status is married filing separately, or if you may be claimed as a dependent on someone else's return. You cannot claim both the tuition and fees deduction and an American opportunity tax credit or lifetime learning credit for the same student in the same tax year. If the educational expenses also qualify as an allowable business expense, then you may be able to claim the tuition and fees deduction in conjunction with a business expense deduction, however you cannot deduct the same expenses twice.

Additionally, you cannot claim a deduction or credit based on expenses paid with tax-free scholarships, fellowships, grants, or education savings account funds, such as a Coverdell education savings account, tax-free savings bond interest, or employer-provided education assistance.

If your modified adjusted gross income exceeds certain limits, your deduction is reduced or eliminated depending on your filing status. You can claim this credit if your modified adjusted gross income is $80,000 or less ($160,000 or less for joint filers).

The Moving Expenses Deduction

The Tax Cuts and Jobs Act has eliminated the moving deduction. The moving expense deduction disappears from the tax year 2018 through the tax year 2025. Consequently, any moving benefits paid in 2018 will now be taxable to the employee.

The One-Half of Self-Employment Tax Deduction

You may be liable for self-employment tax, if you have net self-employment income of $400 or more. You are considered self-employed for tax purposes if you operate a business as a sole proprietor, or if you are an independent contractor. You are also considered self-employed if you are a member of a partnership, or a member of a limited liability company (LLC) that does not elect to be treated as a corporation. The self-employment tax imposed on self-employed persons is basically the equivalent of the combined contributions of the employee and employer, to the Social Security and Medicare tax.

In order to ease the burden of taxation, tax law allows you a deduction of one half of your self-employment tax. You claim this deduction of Schedule 1, line 27. What you are allowed to deduct, essentially, is the employer-equivalent portion of your self-employment tax. Note that this deduction only affects your income tax; it does not affect either your net earnings from self-employment or your self-employment tax.

You must complete Schedule SE, both to figure your self-employment tax, and to take the deduction for half of the tax. You must attach Schedule SE to your tax return.

(Easily available off-the-shelf tax software will effectively complete schedule SE, and compute both the self-employment tax and the deduction, for inclusion on your tax return.)

The Self-Employed Health Insurance Deduction

If you are self-employed, you can take a deduction for all of the health insurance premiums paid for yourself, your spouse, and your dependents. You claim this deduction on Schedule 1, line 29. The amount of the deduction that you can claim, however, cannot exceed your earned income. You are considered self-employed for this deduction if you operate a business or profession as a sole proprietor, if you are a member of a partnership with net earnings from self-employment, or if you are a shareholder receiving wages from an S corporation in which you own more than 2% of the outstanding stock.

To claim this deduction, the following rules apply:

- You <u>must</u> have a net profit for the year.
- You cannot deduct premiums for any month that you (or your spouse) were eligible to participate in an employer-paid health plan.
- You can include long-term care premiums up to the lesser of the amount you pay, or the set amounts, based on your age.
- Your deduction is limited to the **smaller** of: (a) 100% of the cost of your premiums, or your net profit from your business
- Any amount you cannot deduct as an adjustment to income on Form 1040 can be deductible as a medical expense on Schedule A, if you itemize deductions.

The Self-Employed Qualified Retirement Plans Deduction

If you have self-employment income, you can take a tax deduction for contributions you make to a SEP, SIMPLE, or solo 401(k) retirement plan. You claim this deduction on Schedule 1, line 28. You can set up the retirement plan with a financial institution of your choice. If you are a sole proprietor, you'll need an Employer Identification Number, to set up the plan. Each plan has different contribution and deduction rules, and the amount you can deduct will depend on the plan you have.

To qualify for this deduction, you must have self-employment income. Self-employment income for the purpose of this deduction means net profits from a Schedule C or Schedule F (farm income), income from a partnership, or wages received as a shareholder-employee in an S-corporation.

For the 2018 tax year, for example, you could contribute up to $18,500 in deferred salary ($24,500 if you're 50 or older) plus another 25% of your net self-employment earnings after deducting one-half of self-employment tax and contributions for yourself, up to a maximum of $55,000. Contribution limits vary by plan type, and the IRS adjusts the maximums annually. The rules concerning qualified retirement plans are many and complex, so if you believe that you qualify for this deduction, you might need to consult with a credible tax professional, or see IRS Publication 560 for more details

The Health Savings Account Deduction

You can deduct contributions you make to a health savings account (HSA) as an adjustment to income. You claim this deduction on Schedule 1, line 25. A health savings account is a tax-exempt trust or custodial account you can establish with a qualified HSA trustee, to pay or reimburse certain medical expenses for you, your spouse, or your dependents on your tax return.

To be eligible for an HSA deduction, you must meet the following requirements:

- You must be covered under a high deductible health plan (HDHP) and generally have no other health coverage that is not a HDHP.
- You have not enrolled in Medicare.
- You cannot be claimed as a dependent on someone else's tax return.

The benefits of a HSA are as follows:

- All contributions you make are deductible on your tax return, as an adjustment to gross income.
- Any contributions made by your employer are tax free, and will not be included in your gross pay.
- All contributions you make to your HSA can remain in your account from year to year until you use them.
- Interest and earnings on assets in the account are tax-free.
- Distributions are tax-free, provided they are used to pay qualified medical expenses.

Your contributions to a HSA are reported to you on Form 1099-SA.

You report your tax-deductible HSA contributions on IRS Form 8889, Health Savings Accounts, which must be attached to your tax return.

Form 8889 is used for the following purposes:

- To report health savings account (HSA) contributions (including those made on your behalf, and any employer contributions).
- To figure your HSA deduction.
- To report distributions from your HSAs.
- To figure any amounts you may have to include in income, and any additional tax you may owe, if you fail to be an eligible individual.
-
- Note that any distribution from your HSA that is not used for medical expenses will attract an additional tax of 20%.

The Penalty on Early Withdrawal of Savings Deduction

If you withdrew money from a certificate of deposit or other time-deposit savings account prior to your certificate maturing, the financial institution will normally charge you an early withdrawal penalty. This penalty is usually withheld directly from your proceeds from the certificate. This penalty is reported to you on Form 1099-INT, box 2, and is deductible on Schedule 1, line 30, as an adjustment to income. There is no limit on the amount you can deduct.

The Deduction for Business Expenses of Reservists, Performing Artists, and Fee-Based Government Officials

You can deduct certain qualified business expenses directly on your tax return instead of on Schedule A, if you are one of the following professionals:

- A performing artist.
- A member of the National Guard or Reserve.
- A fee-based government official.
-
- Generally, you claim your job-related expenses on Form 2106 or Form 2106-EZ, and transfer them to Schedule A, as an itemized deduction. However, if you are one of these professionals noted above, you can claim your job-related expenses as an adjustment to income, instead of itemizing them on Schedule A. You are allowed to transfer the amounts on Form 2016 or 2106-EZ directly to Schedule 1, line 24.

Reservists

You can deduct expenses incurred for traveling more than 100 miles from your main home if you are a member of the Reserve for the Air Force, Army, Coast Guard, Marine Corps, Navy, Army National Guard, Air National Guard, or Public Health Service Reserve Corps. Your deductible expenses are limited to the federal per diem rates for the city you are traveling to. Performing Artists

You can deduct business expenses if: (a) you provided services in the performing arts for two or more employers, (b) you received at least $200 or more in wages from each employer, (c) your job-related expenses are more than 10% of your income from your performing artist jobs, and (d) you had adjusted gross income of $16,000 or less (without regard to this deduction). You cannot claim this deduction if you are filing MFS.

Fee-Basis Government Officials

If you are a government official who is compensated entirely or partly on a fee basis, your job-related expenses can be deductible.

8 Reporting Self-Employment Income

There is oftentimes a thin line of distinction between a common-law employee and an independent contractor, and this distinction determines how you report income on your tax return. This chapter aims to clarify the distinction between an employee and an independent contractor, and in so doing, also aims to ensure that you gain a thorough understanding of how self-employment income is reported on your tax return, as opposed to how wages are reported. You will also be made aware of the various deductions that you'll be entitled to as a self-employed individual, that you wouldn't normally be eligible for if you were classified as an employee.

Qualified Business Income Deduction

Under the Tax Cuts and Jobs Act, for taxable years beginning after December 31, 2017, taxpayers who operate small business and file Schedule C may be entitled to a deduction of up to 20 percent of their qualified business income from a qualified trade or business. This deduction can be taken in addition to the standard or itemized deductions. Taxpayers with qualified business income (which does not include income from performing services as an employee) and with taxable income under $157,500, or $315,000 for joint returns, will generally be eligible for the deduction.

Self-Employment Income vs. Income from Employment

Before we proceed further, first, we need to make the very important distinction between a common-law employee, an independent contractor, and a self-employed individual.

Common Law Employees vs. Independent Contractors

A common-law employee is a person who performs regular services for an employer who has the right to control and direct the results of the work, and the way in which it is done. For example, the employer: (a) provides the employee's tools, materials, and workplace, and (b) can fire the employee. The employer is required to withhold tax from an employee's wages, and the employee must report these wages directly on Form 1040.

Unlike an employee, an independent contractor does not work regularly for an employer, but works as and when required. Independent contractors are usually paid on a freelance basis. An organization engaged in a trade or business that pays more than $600 to an independent contractor in one year, is required to report this to the IRS as well as to the independent contractor, using Form 1099-MISC. Independent contractors do not have income taxes withheld from their pay as regular employees do. The earnings of a person who is working as an independent contractor, however, are subject to Self-Employment Tax.

The general rule is that an individual is an independent contractor if the payer has the right to control or direct only the result of the work, and not what will be done and how it will be done. Independent contractors report their income initially on Schedule C, Profit or Loss From Business, or Schedule C-EZ, Net Profit From Businesses.

Defining Self-Employed Individuals

A self-employed taxpayer is an individual who is in business for himself or herself, and whose business is not incorporated. You are considered self-employed if the following apply to you:

- You carry on a trade or business as a sole proprietor.
- You are an independent contractor.
- You are a member of a partnership.
- You are in business for yourself in any other way.

An activity qualifies as a business if your primary purpose for engaging in it is for income and profit, and you are involved in the activity with continuity and regularity. Also, an activity generally qualifies to be a business if you have made profits for three years out of the last five years.

If you operate a business, you must report all income earned by the business, even if no reporting document (1099s) is received. You are a sole proprietor if you alone own a business, and the business is not incorporated. Consequently, if you are an independent contractor, you are actually a sole proprietor.

Self-employment income includes the following:

- Income from sole proprietorship and non-employee compensation (Form 1099-Misc).
- Corporate director's fees.
- Partnership income from a partnership operating a business (unless you are a limited partner).
- Guaranteed payments from a partnership (including limited partners).
- Bartering income.
- Real estate rent, if received as a real estate dealer.

101

- Income paid to retired insurance agents based on commissions received prior to retirement.
- Newspaper vendor's income, if vendor is 18 or over.
- Interest received in a trade or business.
- Net earnings of members of the clergy (unless taken a vow of poverty).
- Gains or losses by a dealer in options and commodities.
- A professional fiduciary who administers a deceased person's estate.

The following income is not considered self-employment income:

- Shareholder's share of an S corporation's taxable income.
- Fees received for services performed as a notary public.

Tax law mandates that you <u>must</u> file a tax return if your net earnings from self-employment are at least $400.

Defining Statutory Employees

A distinction must also be made between a self-employed individual and a statutory employee. A statutory employee is a person who is deemed to be an employee by statute. He or she is treated partly as being self-employed, and partly as an employee. Consequently, a statutory employee is: (a) treated as an employee for Social Security and Medicare purposes, and (b) treated as being self-employed for income tax purposes.

An employer should indicate on the worker's Form W-2 (box 13), whether the worker is classified as a statutory employee. Statutory employees report their wages, income, and allowable expenses on Schedule C or C-EZ. Statutory employees are not liable for self-employment tax because their employers must treat them as employees for Social Security and Medicare tax purposes, and withhold these amounts.

Defining Hobby income

A hobby is not considered a business because its activities are not carried on primarily to make a profit. If you earned income from a hobby, you must report that income as Other Income on your tax return. You may report hobby expenses (but only up to the amount of hobby income) as a miscellaneous deduction on Schedule A, if you itemize deductions. If you do not itemize you cannot claim hobby expenses.

How to Report Self-Employment Activities on Schedule C

You must report your income and expenses from self-employment either on Schedule C, or on Schedule C-EZ.

102

You may be eligible to use Schedule C-EZ, which is an abbreviated version of Schedule C, if you have a profit from your business, and:

- Your expenses are not greater than $5,000.
- You have no employees.
- You have no inventory.
- You are not claiming depreciation, or claiming the business use of home deduction.

Your net earnings (or loss) as figured on Schedule C; or your net earnings from Schedule C-EZ, are entered on your tax return. If you own more than one business, you must complete a separate Schedule C or C-EZ for each business. (Note that you cannot use Schedule C-EZ if you have a loss from your business.)

Schedule C is the form used to report your profit or loss from a trade or business, and is broken down into a number of sections, as we shall see below.

The Information Section

You begin completing Schedule C by entering the required information about your business as follows:

- Name of proprietor and social security number.
- Line A – Principal business or profession.
- Line B – Business code. (Your business codes can be found in the 2011 instructions for Schedule C on the IRS website.)
- Line C – Business name.
- Line D – Employer ID number (EIN).
- Line E – Business address.
- Line F – Check the accounting method you are using.

Your accounting method can be one of the following:

(a) The cash method: In using this method, you report income in the year you actually receive the cash, and deduct the expenses in the year you actually pay them.

(b) The accrual method: Under this method, you must report income in the year the sales occur, even if the money is not collected until a later year. Likewise, you report expenses in the year they were incurred, even if you do not pay them until a later year.

(c) The hybrid method: This method is a combination of the cash method and the accrual method.

For lines G through J, you must answer the questions asked by checking the "Yes/No" boxes as appropriate.

The Income Section

Part I

You report your gross income on Part I. You gross income is your total business income, less the cost of goods sold, returns, rebates, and allowances given to customers. You report gross income from your business or from self-employment in Part 1 of Schedule C as follows:

- Gross receipts or sales: This is your total revenue from sales and services. You report them on line 1a and 1b, and total them on line 1d. If you receive non-employee compensation on Form 1099-MISC, report them also on line 1b.
- If you received "statutory employee" income reported to you on Form W-2, include these amounts in the total on line 1c.
- Returns and allowances: This represents the value of any goods and products returned from customers, plus any rebates and allowances given to customers. You report these items on line 2. This amount is subtracted from gross receipts on line 1d.
- Cost of goods sold: This represents the direct cost of the goods that you sold, in order to generate your income. The amount is reported on line 4, but is figured by completing Part III of Schedule C (see below).
- Your gross profit is determined on line 5, by subtracting line 4 from line 3.
- You report any other income on line 6.
- You add lines 5 and 6 to determine your gross income.

If you operate a service business your gross profit will usually be the same as your gross receipts, because you would not keep inventories.

The Expenses Section

Part II

Expenses are business deductions from your income, and you report them on Part II and Part V of Schedule C. Expenses are deductible as long as they are:

- Ordinary expenses: This means expenses that are common and accepted in your type of business.
- Necessary expenses: These are expenses that are appropriate and helpful to your business.

104

The following expenses are specifically required by tax law to be disclosed on Part II of Schedule C:

- **Advertising costs:** These include costs such as classified advertisements, radio and television spots, business cards, mailers and promotional brochures. These costs are reported on line 8.
- **Car and truck expenses:** These are the costs incurred to operate a vehicle for business purposes. In taking this deduction, you have a choice of taking the standard mileage rate, or claiming the actual expenses. You can claim mileage at a standard rate of 54 cents per mile for each business mile traveled. Note, however, that once you begin using the standard mileage rate, you <u>must</u> continue to do so in subsequent years. These costs are reported on line 9.
- **Commissions and fees:** You deduct commissions and fees other than contract labor on line 10.
- **Contract labor:** Any amounts you pay to independent contractors are deducted on line 11.
- **Depletion:** This is a deduction for exhaustible natural resources used up, and is reported on line 12.
- **Depreciation and Section 179 expense:** Depreciation is the process of allocating the cost of fixed assets to the periods in which the assets are used up. This cost is reported on line 13.
- **Employee benefit programs:** These include payments made for employees' accident and health insurance, term life insurance, and dependent care assistance programs. These costs are reported on line 14.
- **Insurance:** All insurance costs (other than health insurance) related to the operation of the business are deducted on line 15.
- **Interest:** Interest on any loans to finance business operations is fully deductible. Mortgage interest on real property used for the business is deducted on line 16a. Any other business interest is deducted on line 16b.
- **Legal and professional fees:** All business related legal and professional fees are deducted on line 17. These include fees for accountants, consultants, attorneys, and amounts paid for tax preparation and advice.
- **Office expenses:** All business related expenses incurred in operating an office are deducted on line 18.
- **Pensions and profit-sharing plans:** Contributions made to employees' pension and profit sharing plans are deducted on line 19.
- **Rent or lease:** Rent or lease payments for motor vehicles, machinery, or equipment used for the business, are deducted on line 20a. Other lease payments for office space, storage, or rent or lease of real property, are deducted on line 20b.

- **Repairs and maintenance:** This includes the costs of labor, supplies, and other items used for the repairs and maintenance of machinery, equipment, and property used in the business. These are deducted on line 21. These costs are fully deductible as long as they do not add to value, or increase the life of the property. You cannot deduct the cost of your own labor.
- **Supplies:** All other supplies that are not covered on line 38 of Part III (see below) are deducted on line 22. These include paper bags, staples, pens and pencils, paper, invoices, etc.
- **Taxes and licenses:** Taxes and licensing fees that are directly related to the business are deductible on line 23.
- **Travel, meals, and entertainment:** Travel expenses are deductible only if they are business related. These are deducted on line 24a. You can deduct <u>only</u> 50% of business related meals and entertainment expenses, and you deduct these expenses on line 24b.
- **Utilities:** Utility costs include gas, electricity, Internet and telephone, trash, and water. As long as these costs are directly related to your business, they are fully deductible on line 25.
- **Wages:** These are the total salaries and wages paid to employees, and are deductible on line 26.
- **Other expenses**: All other business expenses that are not reported on Part II must be listed on Part V. You carry the total of these expenses from line 48 of Part V to line 27a.
- **Total expenses:** You enter the grand total of your business expenses from line 8 through line 27a, on line 28.
- **Business use of your home expenses:** If you use a part of your home for conducting business, you can claim a deduction for the costs relating to the business use of your home on line 30 (see below).

Part III - Cost of goods sold

Cost of goods sold is the direct costs that go into creating or acquiring the products that a business sells; therefore, the only costs to be included are those that are directly tied to the production or acquisition of the products. Cost of goods sold is figured on Part III of Schedule C as follows:

- Enter the value of your inventory (see below) at the beginning of the year on line 35.
- Enter your total purchases less the cost of any items withdrawn for personal use on line 36.
- Enter the cost of any direct labor incurred in producing the goods on line 37. Do not include any amounts that you paid to yourself.
- Enter the costs of any material and supplies involved in producing the goods on line 38.
- Enter any other direct costs on line 39.

- Add the amounts on lines 35 through 39 and enter the result on line 40.
- Enter the value of your inventory at the end of the year on line 41.
- Subtract the amount on line 41 from the amount on line 40 and enter the result on line 42. This is your cost of goods sold for the year, which you transfer to line 4 of Part 1.

Inventories: On line 33, you must check the method you used to value your inventories. Inventories can be valued at cost, or lower of cost or market. Either of two methods can be used to determine cost at the beginning and at the end of the year:

(a) The FIFO (first in, first out) method: This method assumes that the products which are purchased first are sold first.

(b) The LIFO (last in, first out) method: This method assumes that the products that are purchased last are considered sold first.

Part IV – Information on your vehicle
Complete this part only if you are claiming car or truck expenses on line 9, and are not required to file Form 4562 for your business.

Part V – Other Expenses
All expenses not covered on lines 8 to 26, and line 30 of Part II, are listed on Part V.
You carry the total expenses from line 48 of Part V to line 27a of Part II.

The Net Profit or Loss Section

This is where you compute the net profit (or loss) from your business. This amount is figured by first subtracting the total expenses on line 28 from the gross income on line 7, to compute **Tentative Profit of Loss**, on line 29. If you claim the business use of home deduction, subtract the amount on line 30 from the amount on line 29, to compute **Net Profit or Loss** on line 31. Otherwise, transfer the amount on line 29 to line 31. You transfer the amount on line 31 to your tax return.

(Easily available off-the-shelf tax software will effectively facilitate the process of completing Schedule C, and will take care of all the necessary additions and subtractions.)

How to Claim the Business Use of Home Deduction

If you use a part of your home for conducting business, you can claim a Business Use of Home Deduction.

Two qualifying tests must be met to claim the business use of home deduction: the principal place of business test and the regular and exclusive test.

The principal place of business test is met if you use a portion of your home for business and the following hold true:

(a) You use your home as your principal place of business.
(b) Your home is the place of business where your patients, clients, or customers meet with you in the normal course of business.
(c) You use a portion of your home to conduct administrative and managerial functions, and your business does not have another fixed location from which to carry out these functions.

The regular and exclusive use test states that the home office must be used exclusively for your business, and on a regular basis. Failing to meet either of these conditions will result in the disallowance of a home office deduction. Exclusive use means the taxpayer must use this portion of the home only for business purposes; there is to be no other use of the space. Regular use means the taxpayer must use this portion of the home in the business activity on a continuing basis. Note however, that you do not have to use the entire room exclusively for your home office; you can separate a part of the room for this use. Note also, that qualifying day-care providers are exempt from the exclusive use test.

You have two choices for calculating your home office deduction: the standard method and the simplified option, and you don't have to use the same method every year. To use the simplified option, your home office must not be larger than 300 square feet, and you cannot deduct depreciation or home-related itemized deductions. The simplified option lets you multiply an IRS-determined rate by your home office square footage.

The standard method requires you to calculate your actual home office expenses. With the standard method, when figuring the amount you can deduct for the business use of your home, you must first of all determine the amount of your home expenses that can be attributable to the portion of the home used in your business. This essentially depends on what percentage of the home you use for business. To figure this percentage, you may divide the square footage used for business, by the square footage of the entire home.

In addition to the square footage percentage, day care operators must also figure the percentage of time the portion of their home was used for day-care activities. This is determined by dividing total number of hours used for day-care activities, by the total number of hours available during the year.

For a detached garage or other separate structure, the rule of the law is less stringent, and the only requirement is that the building is used in connection with your trade or business. You can also claim deductions if you use an area of your home for storage of inventory or product samples.

You report the expenses for home-office deduction on Form 8829, as either direct expenses or indirect expenses.

> Direct expenses: These are those expenses that relate solely to the part of your home that you use for business; for example, painting the home office, or repairing the home office floor.

> Indirect expenses: These are the expenses that relate to running the home as a whole, and these include mortgage interest, real estate taxes, roof repairs, etc. A portion of these expenses must be apportioned to the home office, based on the square footage percentage.

The amount of your deduction is figured on Form 8829, Expenses for Business Use of Your Home, and entered on line 30 of Schedule C. This amount is deducted from your tentative profit on line 29, and results in your profit or loss on line 31, which you report on Form 1040.

(Easily available off-the-shelf tax software will effectively complete Form 8829, and compute the deduction for inclusion on your tax return.)

How to Report Form 1099-K for Business

Businesses that accept credit and debit cards when making sales to customers will receive an IRS tax Form 1099-K, Merchant Card and Third-Party Payments, from their credit card processing company. The Form 1099-K will report the total payment transactions for the year. The reporting requirement is part of on-going government efforts to increase collection of income tax. Basically, banks that issue credit cards, and other vendors that handle third party payments, with Paypal perhaps being the best known, will have to track the quantity and dollar amount of payments made to each recipient.

For any recipient that receives payments from a particular bank or third-party vendor that surpass two specific thresholds, that bank or third-party will be required to report total payments for the calendar year on Form 1099-K. The two calendar-year thresholds that must both be met are: (a) a total of at least 200 transactions, and (b) at least $20,000 in total payments. If you meet these thresholds, banks or third party payment processors, are required to fill out and provide a Form 1099-K to the government. That way, the government can then compare it to what you are actually reporting. If you have gross sales of less than $20,000 a year or fewer than 200 transactions, then Form 1099-K reporting will not be necessary.

For those who have been under-reporting their income, this could mean significant changes for you. If you don't fully report your income, you might find yourself coming under audit pressure if the Form 1099-K indicates that you make more than the sales you actually report.

How to Figure Self-Employment Tax

Self-employment tax is a tax consisting of Social Security and Medicare tax, which is primarily imposed on individuals who work for themselves. It is similar to the Social Security and Medicare taxes withheld from the pay of most wage earners. A self-employed individual is considered both the employer and the employee, so a self-employed person pays both halves of the tax. Generally, the rate of the tax is 15.3%, composed of a Social Security tax of 12.4% on the first $118,500 of net self-employment income, and a Medicare tax of 2.9% on all net self-employment income. You figure your self-employment tax by completing Schedule SE, Self-Employment Tax.

How to Complete Schedule SE

If you have net earnings from self-employment of $400 or more, or if you have church employee income of $108.28 or more, you are required to file a tax return and pay self-employment tax. You are required to file Schedule SE with your tax return.

If you are reporting only self-employment income, you must use Section A, which is the short form of Schedule SE. If you are reporting both W-2 income and self-employed income, you must use Section B, the long form of Schedule SE.

Self-employment tax is computed on line 5 of Section A of Schedule SE, or on line 12 of Section B. This amount is reported on your tax return and included with your other taxes payable. Remember that tax law allows one half of your self-employment taxes as a deduction from income.

(Easily available off-the-shelf software will effectively complete Schedule SE, and compute the amount of self-employment tax for inclusion on your tax return.)

How to Figure Clergy Self-Employment Tax

If you are a member of the clergy, tax law allows you to exclude from your income, the fair rental value of a parsonage, or a housing allowance received. This exclusion, however, is only for income tax purposes; no exclusion applies for self-employment tax purposes. For Social Security and Medicare tax purposes, a duly ordained, licensed or commissioned minister is considered self-employed. Consequently, this means that all your income; that is, your salary on Form W-2, your net profit on Schedule C or C-EZ, and your housing allowance, less your employee business expenses, are subject to self-employment tax on Schedule SE. Members of a religious order who have taken a vow of poverty are not subject to self-employment tax on earnings for performing duties by the order.

Deducting a Net Operating Loss (NOL)

When you have a business and your expenses exceed your income for the year, you may have a net operating loss (NOL) for the year, and this is deducted from your other income (if any). After preparing your tax return, if the amount on line 41 is a negative number, you should use Form 1045 to determine the allowable NOL.

For tax years beginning before January 1, 2018, NOLs were able to offset 100% of taxable income. They were allowed to be carried back two years and carried forward for twenty years. Under the new law, an NOL can offset only 80% of taxable income in any given tax year. Furthermore, NOLs can no longer be carried back; they must be carried forward. The old 20-year carry-forward period has been replaced with an indefinite carry-forward period

You claim the NOL in each carry-forward year by deducting the amount of the loss as a negative number on the Other Income line on your tax return. You must attach a statement, which explains how you computed the NOL carry forward.

Husband and Wife Businesses

Generally, if a husband and wife own an unincorporated business together and share in the profits and losses, the business is defined as a partnership for tax purposes, even if there is no formal partnership agreement. This means, then, that the taxpayer and spouse should file Form 1065 (a partnership return) separately from their personal return, along with a separate Schedule K-1 for each spouse. The information from the Schedule K-1s would then be entered into the personal tax return.

The Small Business and Work Opportunity Tax Act of 2007, however, provides an exception to this rule, and states that a business venture whose **only** members are a husband and a wife filing a joint return, can elect **not** to be treated as a partnership for federal tax purposes.

If the taxpayer and spouse meet the following requirements, they can file a joint return and include a separate Schedule C for each spouse:

- Both spouses must materially participate in the business.
- The spouses are the only owners of the business,
- The spouses must file a joint return, **and**
- The spouses must make an affirmative election to be treated as a joint venture.

The spouses make this election simply by filing a joint Form 1040 tax return, with each spouse filing a separate Schedule C, dividing all items of income, gain, loss, deduction, and credit between them in accordance with each spouse's respective interest in the joint venture.

How to Report Farm Income or Loss

If you operate a farm, you must report your self-employment income and expenses from your farming business, on Schedule F, Profit or Loss from Farming. Schedule F is to be used only for farmers who are considered sole proprietors. Farmers who operate their farming business through a corporation or other business entity must report income and expenses on the appropriate business tax return for that type of business structure.

Gross income from farming usually consists of income from cultivating the soil, or raising agricultural commodities, and includes the following:

- Income from operating a stock, dairy, poultry, bee, or fruit farm.
- Income from a plantation, ranch, nursery, range, orchard, or oyster bed.
- Crop shares for the use of land.
- Gains from sales of draft, breeding, dairy, or sporting livestock.

How to Complete Schedule F

You use Schedule F to report your farming income and expense by completing the sections listed below.

Information section: You must enter the following in the information section:

- Name of the proprietor.
- Social Security number.
- Principal crop or activity.
- The activity code (from part IV of Schedule F).
- The accounting method (whether cash or accrual).
- The employer identification number (EIN).

- On lines E to G, check the appropriate "Yes" or "No" boxes.

Part I: If you are using the cash method, enter total farm income on lines 1 through 8, separating non-taxable income from taxable income. You figure gross income on line 9, by totaling the amounts on lines 1 through 8.

Part II: Enter total farm expenses (whether you use cash or accrual method) on lines 10 through 32. Expenses are totaled on line 33 and subtracted from gross income on line 9 to figure net farm profit or loss on line 34.

Part III: If you are using the accrual method, you must not complete Part 1 of Schedule F. Instead, you enter your total farm income on lines 37 through 43 of Part III. You figure your cost of sales on lines 45 through 48, taking into account opening and closing inventories. You figure gross income on line 50 by subtracting line 49 from line 44, and transfer the result to line 9 of Part 1.

You enter your profit or loss figured on line 34 on your tax return, and also on Schedule SE, to figure your self-employment tax. If you have a loss, you must complete lines 35 and 36 of Schedule F before entering the amount, and follow the instructions, as the amount of the loss that you can deduct may be limited.

(Easily available off-the-shelf tax software will effective complete Schedule F, and calculate self-employment tax for inclusion on your tax return.)

Types of Farm Income Not Reported on Schedule F

Certain types of farm income are not reported on Schedule F, but must be reported on some other schedule or form. These are as follows:

(a) Income from providing agricultural services such as soil preparation, veterinary, farm labor, horticultural, or management for a fee or on a contract basis. You must report income from these sources on Schedule C or C-EZ.

(b) Income from breeding, raising, or caring for dogs, cats, or other pet animals. You must report income from these sources on Schedule C or C-EZ.

(c) Sales of livestock held for draft, breeding, sport, or dairy purposes. You must report this income on Form 4797, and then report the gain or loss on your tax return.

(d) Income from farm rental. This must be reported on Form 4835, Farm Rental Income and Expenses, and then on Schedule E.

The Estimated Tax Requirement for Farmers

If you receive at least two-thirds of your gross income from farming or fishing for the current or previous tax years, you are only required to make one estimated tax payment. The due date for this payment is January 15th of the next year, but if you file your tax return by March 1 of the next year and pay all taxes owed, no estimated payment is required.

Some Tax Advantages for Farmers

Farmers are very fortunate, in that they can enjoy special tax advantages that are not available to other taxpayers. Some of these special advantages are the following:

> **Weather-related conditions sale**: If you were forced to sell livestock or poultry due to weather-related conditions, you can elect to report the income from the sale in the year following the year of the sale. The amount to be postponed, however, must be based on the additional number of livestock that were sold solely because of the weather-related conditions.

> **Crop insurance and disaster payments**: You normally include these types of payments received in income. You may however postpone reporting these proceeds until the following year, if it can be proved that the crops which were subject to the disaster would indeed have been sold in the following year, were it not for the disaster.

> **Income averaging**: If you are engaged in a farming business, you may be able to average all or some of your farm income, by allocating it to the three prior years. Income averaging helps to even out the tax burden if you have widely varying income from one year to the next, for example, little income one year and huge income the next. The tax liability can be spread out over a three-year period; instead of being all due in the year the high income was earned.

There are a number of other tax advantages available for farmers, so if you earn a substantial amount of your income from farming, you should probably take some time to read IRS Publication 225, Farmer's Tax Guide, to see what addition tax benefits you may be eligible for.

Tax Planning for Schedule C filers

Schedule C filers are more prone to IRS audits than any other category of taxpayers. This is especially so if your self-employment activity is your only source of income. You must therefore make every effort to report your income and expenditure as accurately as possible. Consistently showing a loss on a Schedule C return raises a huge red flag for an IRS audit, because if you are consistently reporting losses from your business, and have no other source of income, the IRS is going to ask this infamous question: How do you live? Unless you can properly prove your position, you can be hit with adjustments and penalties, including what the IRS calls an "accuracy related penalty" which is a whopping 20% of the taxes understated, as computed by the IRS.

The importance of proper record keeping by Schedule C filers therefore cannot be overemphasized. You have a responsibility to ensure that all your business related records for each year are properly filed away and kept in a safe place for a period of at least three years. If you cannot provide legitimate supporting evidence such as suppliers' invoices and contracts, to prove your expenses, the IRS will disallow these expenses, and you will be subject to adjustments, penalties, and interest.

9 Reporting Real Estate Rental, and Other Schedule E Income

Schedule E, Supplemental Income and Loss, is the tax schedule used to report income and expenses arising from real estate rental, royalties, or from pass-through entities (like trusts, estates, partnerships, or S corporations.

Overview of Schedule E

Schedule E is divided into a number of parts, and you complete each part as follows:

Part I
You report income (loss) from real estate rental and income from royalties, on Part I of Schedule E. You deduct all expenses and operating costs from this income, to determine your net gain or loss from real estate and royalty activities.

Part I of Schedule E can accommodate up to three rental properties, and you complete as follows:

- On line 1, you enter the type, and the address of each real estate property rented.
- For each rented property, if you or your family used it during the tax year for personal purposes, you must state on line 2 the number of days the property was used for personal purposes.
- You report gross rental/royalty income on line 3a or 3b, as appropriate.
- You enter your rental expenses on lines 5 through 19.
- If any of your real estate/royalty loss is deductible, you enter it on line 25.
- You figure your total real estate rental and royalty income (or loss) on line 26.

Part II
This is where you report income or loss from partnerships and S corporations.

Part III
You report income or loss from estates and trusts in this section.

Part IV

You report income or loss from Real Estate Mortgage Investment Conduits in this section.

Part V

This is the summary of all your Schedule E income; the total computed on line 41 is transferred to Form 1040.

Reporting Real Estate Rental Income

Rental income is any payment you receive for the use or occupation of real property. If you rented out residential or commercial real estate during the year, you will normally report your income and expenses from this activity on Part I of Schedule E. Your net income (or loss, in certain cases) from real estate activities is reported on Form 1040. If you have more than three rental properties, you must complete as many Schedules E as are needed; then combine the totals on one Schedule E. You must attach all your Schedules E to your tax return.

You are required to report rental income on your tax return for the year you actually or constructively receive the income. Note that you constructively receive income when it is made available to you, for example, by being credited to your bank account. Any income you receive from the rental of residential or nonresidential real estate is rental income, and must be included in your gross income.

In addition to the actual rental payments you receive, the following amounts received from tenants must also be included in rental income:

Advance Rent

This is any amount you receive before the period that it covers. You must include advance rent in your rental income in the year you receive it, regardless of the period covered, or the accounting method you use.

Cancellation of Lease Payments

If a tenant pays you to cancel a lease, this money is also considered rental income, and must be reported in the year you receive it.

Expenses Paid by Tenants

You must include in rental income, any expenses paid by a tenant and deducted from subsequent rental payments. If your tenant pays any of your expenses in lieu of rent, these payments are regarded as rental income. For example, if your tenant pays the water and sewage bill for your rental property and deducts it from the normal rent payment, you must treat the amount of the expenses paid by your tenant as rental income. You can deduct these expenses, however, if they qualify as deductible rental expenses.

Property and Services Received in Lieu of Rent

If you receive property or services, instead of rent money, you are required to include the fair market value of the property or services received, as part of your rental income. If the services are provided at an agreed upon or specified price, that price must be treated as the fair market value, unless there is evidence to the contrary. For example, if your tenant offers to do repairs to your rental property instead of paying 2 months' rent; you must include in your rental income the amount the tenant would have paid for 2 months' rent. You can include that same amount as a rental expense for repairs to your property.

Security deposits

You are required to include in rental income, any security deposit that is not returned to a tenant, and any security deposit intended to be utilized as the last month's rent. Do not include a security deposit in your income if you plan to return it to your tenant at the end of the lease. But if you keep part or all of the security deposit during any year, because your tenant does not live up to the terms of the lease, you must include the amount that you keep, in your income for that year. If an amount called a security deposit is to be used as a final payment of rent, it is actually advance rent, and must be included in your income when you receive it.

Reporting Real Estate Rental Expenses

Any expenses that you incur for your rental property can be deducted from gross rental income. You generally deduct your rental expenses in the year you pay them. Below are some of the main categories of expenses that are usually associated with rental property.

Repairs

You can deduct the cost of repairs that you make to your rental property. However, you may <u>not</u> deduct the cost of improvements; this cost is recovered through depreciation (see below). The distinction between repairs and improvements is as follows:

> (a) A repair keeps your property in good operating condition but does not materially add value to the property. Some examples of repairs are: painting, fixing leaks and cracks, and replacing broken doors or windows.

> (b) An improvement adds to the value of your property, prolongs its useful life, or adapts it to new uses. Examples of improvements are: adding a room, a deck, a fence, or a new roof.

Auto and Travel Expenses

You can also deduct your related auto and travel expenses, if the main purpose of the travel is to collect rental income, or to manage or maintain the rental property.
- If you travel away from your home, you can deduct 50% of the cost of your meals.
- If you use your personal vehicle for rental related purposes, you can deduct the expense using either the standard mileage rate, or the actual expenses incurred.
- You must keep written records of all your travel expenses, and must be able to allocate expenses between rental and non-rental activities.

Depreciation

Depreciation is a deduction that many people earning real estate rental income often overlook on their tax returns. You are entitled to deduct an amount for depreciation of your property used in a rental activity. This is a yearly deduction for some or all of what you paid for your property, and which reduces your taxable rental income.

You can also claim a depreciation deduction for certain other property, such as appliances, furniture, carpets, etc., that is used in the rental property. These items are depreciated over 5 years. Note however, that you cannot claim a Section 179 deduction for property used in rental activities.

Other Deductible Expenses

In addition to repairs, auto expenses, and depreciation, the following expenses are also deductible:

- Advertising for renters.
- Cleaning and maintenance.
- Commissions or management fees.
- Insurance premiums.
- Local transportation expenses to oversee the property.
- Legal expenses concerning the rental property.
- Mortgage interest.
- Real estate taxes.
- Supplies.
- Tax return preparation for rental forms.
- Utilities.

Deductibility of Vacant Property Expenses

Tax law also allows you to deduct certain expenses for rental property even while the property is vacant, as long as the property was available for rent during that period. You may deduct all ordinary and necessary rental expenses incurred from the time you make the property available for rent, until the time the property is either rented or sold. Ordinary and necessary expenses for vacant rental properties are the costs of managing, conserving and maintaining the property. All expenses incurred and paid in connection with managing and maintaining the property while it is vacant are deductible. However, you cannot deduct the loss of rental income during the period in which the property is vacant.

Expenses for Rental Property Also Used for Personal Use

If your rental property is sometimes used for personal purposes, you must divide the expenses between rental use and personal use, and the expenses you can deduct may be limited (see below).

Providing Significant Services for Tenants

If you provide significant services for your tenant's convenience (for example, cleaning, providing food, etc.), this is considered operating a business, so you must report your income and expenses on Schedule C or C-EZ, instead of on Schedule E.

Change of Property from Personal Use to Rental Use

If you change your property from personal use to rental use after the beginning of the year, you must allocate the expenses between rental and personal use as follows:

- The cost to be used for the depreciation deduction for the rental use portion of the property is the **lesser** of: (a) the fair market value of the property on the date it is changed to rental use, or (b) the adjusted basis (cost) of the property.
- You deduct all rental expenses on Schedule E, including mortgage interest and taxes, relating to the period <u>after</u> the property has been placed in rental use.
- Mortgage interest and taxes (but not depreciation and insurance) incurred for the period during which the property was in personal use, may be deducted as an itemized deduction on Schedule A.

Part of Property Rented and Part for Personal Use

If you rent part of your property and use part for personal purposes, you must divide the expenses as if you had two separate pieces of property. Expenses must be allocated as follows:

- Expenses for the rental part of the property may be deducted from rental income on Schedule E. You can deduct as a rental expense the entire amount of expenses that relate <u>solely</u> to the rental part of the property, for example, painting or repairing the flooring of the rented section.
- For expenses such as mortgage interest and property taxes, you can deduct a part of these as rental expenses on Schedule E, and the balance as personal expenses on Schedule A, if you itemize deductions.
- You can deduct depreciation <u>only</u> on the rental part of the property.
- You can use any reasonable method to divide expenses; the most common method used is square footage percentage.

Personal Use of a Vacation Home or Dwelling Unit

If you rented out a vacation home or other dwelling unit, and also used it for personal purposes, you must divide your expenses between rental use and personal use. If your expenses for rental use are more than your rental income, you will not be able to deduct all of the rental expenses. Dwelling units include houses, apartments, condominiums, mobile homes, boats, and similar property.

The following rules apply if there is any personal use of this type of property:

- The amount of expenses you can deduct for rental use is limited to the days the property is actually rented.
- If you use the dwelling unit as a home, you are also limited in the deductions that you can take.

Tax law states that you use a dwelling unit as a home if you used it for personal purposes more than the **greater** of:

- 14 days, or
- 10% of the total days it is rented at a fair rental price.

If you do not use your rental unit as a home, as defined by tax law (less than 14 days or 10% of days rented), you must report all rental income, and deduct all rental expenses, as you would with any other rental property.

If your dwelling unit was used as a home, as determined above, you must figure your income and deductions as follows:

- If the property was rented for less than 15 days during the year, you must **not** report any rental income, and must **not** deduct any rental expenses. In other words, you must not include any of this rental activity on your tax return.
- If the property was rented for 15 days or more, you must report all rental income, but divide expenses between personal use and rental use, based on the number of days used for each purpose.
- You can deduct expenses **only** to the amount that is equal to your gross rental income from the property. Rental expenses exceeding gross rental income must be carried forward to the next year (no loss deduction is allowed).

A day of personal use of a dwelling unit is any day it is used by:

- You or any other person who has an ownership interest in it.
- A member of your family, unless the family member uses the dwelling as his or her main home and pays a fair rental price. For this purpose, family members include only: brothers, sisters, half-brothers, half-sisters, spouses, ancestors (parents, grandparents, etc.) and lineal descendants (children, grandchildren, etc.).
- Anyone under an arrangement that lets you use some other dwelling unit.
- Any who rents it at less than a fair rental price.

Any day spent working substantially full time repairing and maintaining the property is not counted as a day of personal use, even if family members use the property for recreational purposes on the same day. For purposes of determining if the dwelling unit was used as a home, count as a day of personal use any day you used it for personal purposes while it was rented.

If the dwelling unit is your main home, do not count as personal use days, the days before or after it was rented if:

- You rented or tried to rent the property for 12 or more consecutive months, or
- You rented or tried to rent the property for a period of less than 12 consecutive months, and the period ended because you sold or exchanged the property.

Reporting Not-For-Profit Rental

Not-for-profit rental property is property that is rented at less than the fair rental price for the property. You report not-for-profit rental income and expenses as follows:

- You report your income directly on Form 1040 as Other Income; you cannot use Schedule E to report not-for-profit rental.
- You can only deduct expenses that do not exceed income, and you can do so only on Schedule A, if you itemize deductions.
- You can carry forward any expenses that exceed income, and deduct them in future years when you have similar income to set them off against.

Limited Deductibility of Real Estate Losses

Real estate rental is considered income from a passive activity. A passive activity is a business activity in which the investor or business owner has the potential to profit, but in which the individual does not materially or physically participate. Consequently, real estate losses are considered a passive activity loss. The amount of real estate loss that you can deduct from your other (non-passive income) is limited by the at risk rules, and the passive activity rules.

At Risk Rules

Losses from passive activities are first subject to at-risk rules. At-risk rules limit your deductible losses from most real estate property placed in service after 1986. Property placed in service before 1987 are not subject to at-risk rules.

At-risk rules state that:

- Any deductible loss from an activity subject to at-risk rules cannot exceed the amount of money or property you have at risk at the end of the year.
- You are considered at risk to the extent of your cash investment; that is, the cost (adjusted basis) of any other property contributed to the activity, and loans for which you are personally liable.

Passive Activities Rules

Rental activities are considered passive activities, and the general rule is that you cannot offset your real estate losses against your other (non-passive) income. Generally, real estate losses should be carried forward and offset against future real estate income, but there is an exception to this rule (see below).

Exception to the Passive Activities Rules
Tax law allows an exception to the passive activities rule, as far as rental property is concerned: If you actively participated in a passive rental activity, you may be able to deduct a special loss allowance of up to $25,000, from your non-passive income, subject to the following conditions:

- You are considered to have actively participated in the rental activity if you own at least 10% of the rental property, and are responsible for making significant and bona fide management decisions. Management decisions include approving new tenants, deciding on rental terms, approving expenditures, and similar decisions.

- Note however, that the special loss allowance is reduced to a maximum of $12,500, if you used the MFS filing status, and lived apart from your spouse all of the year. No special loss allowance is available if you filed MFS and live with your spouse at any time during the year.

- The special allowance begins to phase-out at AGI over $100,000 ($50,000 if filing MFS and lived apart from spouse; $0 if lived with spouse). Taxpayers with adjusted gross incomes above $150,000 may not take the deduction at all.

-

Real Estate Professionals

If you materially participated in real estate activities as a real estate professional, your rental activity is **not** considered a passive activity, and there is no limit on the amount of real estate rental losses that you can deduct from your other income. You qualify to be a real estate professional, however, only if you meet the following two basic tests:

- The time spent in performing services in real property trades or businesses is more than the time spent in performing all other income earning activities.
- You spent more than 750 hours performing real estate activities for the year.

It is very important to note that anyone who claims this status usually becomes an easy target or IRS audits. Your best defense, then, is to adequately document all of your real estate activities, however minor. Anyone looking to claim this classification should be keeping a detailed log of dates, locations and activities, which should preferably be backed up with photographs or other evidence showing that you are actually working in this activity.

The Tax Advantages of Investing in Real Estate

For both middle and high-income individuals alike, the tax advantages of investing in real estate can be substantial. Some of the advantages are as follows:

Depreciation: The IRS allows investors to depreciate (deduct from rental income) the cost of a residential rental building over a period of 27.5 years, and 39 years for nonresidential property. Moreover, all capital improvements that add to the value of a building, and have a useful life of one year or more, are also depreciable. The more you invest in real estate, the greater tax deduction you can take.

Tax deferral: Gains you make from real estate investments are not taxed until you sell the property. For example, if you purchase a home for $150,000 and it appreciates to $200,000, the $50,000 gain is protected from taxes until you sell the property. This allows your investment to grow tax-free year after year, further compounding its growth.

Capital Gains tax rate: A capital gain is the profit realized from selling an asset. A capital gain is taxed at a lower rate than ordinary income, and is currently at a maximum rate of 20%. When you sell real estate, you will enjoy this lower rate of tax on your profits, and there is no limit on the amount of capital gains subject to this reduced tax rate.

Tax Deferred Exchange: Even though capital gains tax rates are relatively low, you can avoid them altogether by doing a Section 1031 exchange, also called a like-kind or tax-deferred exchange. A tax-deferred exchange allows investors to reinvest the money coming out of a sale of real estate property into the purchase of another one. As long as all the money is reinvested in like-kind property, no taxes are paid on the profit earned on the sale. There is no limit to the number of exchanges you can do, but strict time frames apply to the transactions.

Tax deduction advantages: Finance and operating costs such as mortgage interest, property management fees, property taxes, repair and maintenance -- all these charges can be claimed as deductions from your real estate rental income.

Other Schedule E Income

Apart from reporting real estate activities, Schedule E is also used by taxpayers to report royalties, and income or losses from partnerships, S-corporations, and other pass-through entities, where gains and losses "pass through" to partners or stockholders.

Royalties

Royalties are payments you receive for granting another person the right to exploit certain intellectual or investment property that you own. Note however, that royalties that are derived as a result of your creative work, is considered self-employment income, and are reported on Schedule C or C-EZ, instead of on Schedule E.

Any royalties derived from investment activities in mineral interest, such as a patent or right to extract natural resources, are reported on Schedule E. The following rules apply:

- The payer of more than $10 in royalties should send you a Form 1099-MISC.
- You report royalty income and expenses on Part 1 of Schedule E.
- If you are in business as a self-employed writer or artist, you must report your royalties on Schedule C or C-EZ, instead of on Schedule E.

Partnership and S Corporation Income

You use Part II of Schedule E for reporting income and losses from partnerships and S corporations. After deducting expenses from income, the company's or partnership's net earnings pass through to its shareholders or partners. The profit or loss from the company or partnership is reported on Schedule K-1, which is mailed annually to each shareholder or partner. Passive income and losses must be separated from non-passive income and losses, and the passive activities rules applied.

Income from Estates and Trusts

Estates and trusts often generate income before the principal is distributed to the beneficiaries. Income and losses from estates and trusts are reported on Form1041, and the taxpayer receiving this form carries the amounts forward to Part III of Schedule E. As with Part II, passive income is separated from non-passive income. Passive income is income generated without the taxpayer's active or material participation in the activity producing the income.

Income and Losses from Real Estate
Mortgage Investment Conduits

Income and losses from Real Estate Mortgage Investment Conduits or REMICs,
are reported on Part IV of Schedule E. Individual taxpayers who have invested in "bundles" of mortgages, report their income here.

10 How to Claim Your Depreciation Deductions

Depreciation is an income tax deduction that unfortunately is oftentimes overlooked. It is a deduction that allows a taxpayer to recover the cost or other basis of certain property used in business or rental activity, over a certain period of time. It is an annual allowance that the taxpayer receives for the wear and tear, deterioration, or obsolescence of the property. Most types of tangible property used in business (except land) such as buildings, machinery, vehicles, furniture, and equipment, are depreciable. Likewise, certain intangible property, such as patents, copyrights, and computer software, are also depreciable.

When you purchase investment and income producing property (machinery, equipment, motor vehicles, buildings, etc.) that have a useful life lasting substantially beyond the tax year, you generally cannot deduct the total cost of this property from your taxable income in the year you acquire them. Tax law allows you, however, to recover the cost of these assets, by taking yearly deductions for depreciation over the life of the property. Depreciation, then, is the tax deduction to compensate for the decrease in the value of property, over the time it is used in the business.

Before we go any further, we must make a distinction between real and personal property:

- Real property is any investment in real estate (land and buildings).
- Personal property is any other property that is not real property (machinery, equipment, cars, furniture, computers, etc.).

The form or schedule you use to report your depreciation deductions depends on the activity that the property being depreciated is being used in. For example, if you are using your property in your self-employed business, you will report your depreciation deductions on Schedule C. If you are using your real property in rental activities, you will report your depreciation deductions on Schedule E.

You can depreciate property ONLY if:

- You use it for business, or hold it to produce income.
- You expect it to last for more than one year.

- It has a limited useful life. (That is why land is never depreciated; land has an infinite life).

You cannot take a depreciation deduction for the following types of property:

- Real or personal property that you use for personal (non-business) purposes.
- Land.
- Items placed in service and disposed of in the same year.
- Most leased property.
- Inventory or stock in trade.

There are additional rules and requirements for depreciating property that is likely to be used for both personal and business purposes (see listed property below).

Claiming the Depreciation Deduction

As already defined, depreciation is the process of allocating the cost of an asset to the periods in which the asset is used. This is done by taking yearly depreciation deductions over its expected useful life, against income earned each year. To claim a depreciation deduction, the following rules apply:

- You must own the property and use it in your business, or you must otherwise use it for producing income.
- The depreciation deduction must be a percentage of the basis (cost) of the property, and it must be claimed over the useful life of the property.
- Both the percentage rates and the useful lives of each category of property are determined by IRS rules.
- If your property is depreciable, you must take the depreciation deductions.

You can claim a depreciation deduction for both tangible and intangible property.

- Tangible property comprises of property that you can physically see or touch, and includes all real and personal property. Tangible property includes buildings, machinery, equipment, motor vehicles, furniture, computers, etc.
- Intangible property is generally property that cannot be seen or touched, but which has value. Intangible property includes goodwill, certain computer software, copyrights, patents, etc.

When to Begin Taking Depreciation Deductions

You should begin taking depreciation deductions when you place property in service for use in your trade or business. Property is considered placed in service when it is ready and available for its specific use, which basically means, when the asset is in the position and location that makes it ready for use in your business.

When to Stop Taking Depreciation deductions

You must stop claiming depreciation for your property after you have fully recovered its cost, or when you retire the property from service, whichever comes first.

- Cost in property is fully recovered when your depreciation deductions (including any Section 179 deduction claimed) are equal to your cost or investment in the property.

- Property is retired from service when you permanently withdraw it from use in your trade or business, or from use in the production of income.

Defining Depreciation Systems

There are basically two depreciation systems currently being used in the United States:
The Modified Accelerated Cost Recovery System (MACRS), and the Accelerated Cost Recovery System (ACRS). MACRS replaced ACRS in 1986, and is the depreciation system used for most property placed in service after December 31, 1986.

Under these systems, the taxpayer recovers the cost (basis) of business property over a specified period of time, by claiming annual deductions for depreciation. The particular system of depreciation that you will use to figure your depreciation deduction depends basically on: (a) the type of property, and (b) when it was placed in service. Generally, if you are depreciating property you placed in service before 1987, you must ACRS. For property placed in service after 1986, you generally must use MACRS.

For each category of property, the IRS provides MACRS and ACRS tables that give the depreciation rate (the percentage of the cost you can deduct) for each year the property is in use.

To deduct depreciation, you can use either a straight-line method, or you can use an accelerated method.

- The straight-line method of depreciation provides equal deductions for each year of useful life.
-
- Accelerated methods allow you larger deductions during the early years, thus resulting in faster recovery of the cost of the property.

The depreciation method that you use for any particular asset is fixed at the time you first place the asset into service, and thus cannot be changed. So, whatever rules or tables are in effect for that year must be followed as long as you own the property.

The Modified Accelerated Cost Recovery System (MACRS)

You are required to use the MACRS system to depreciate most tangible depreciable property placed in service after 1986. You must also use MACRS to depreciate real property acquired before 1987 that you changed from personal use to business or income-producing use after 1986.

MACRS cannot be used to depreciate the following types of property:

- Intangible property.
- Films, videotapes and recordings.
- Certain real and personal property placed in service before 1987.

MACRS essentially consists of two systems:

- General Depreciation System (GDS). This system is a combination of accelerated methods and the straight-line method. You use this system to depreciate most tangible property.
- Alternative Depreciation System (ADS). You use this system when you are specifically required by law to use it, or when you elect to use it. The ADS is essentially a straight-line method, and must be used in certain situations when normal MACRS is not allowed.

Depreciation calculations are based on the MACRS percentage tables, which incorporate the different depreciation conventions (see below). To effectively claim your depreciation deduction under MACRS, you need to know the following information about your property:

- Its basis (cost).
- The property class it belongs to.
- Its recovery period.

- The date it was placed in service.
- The convention to use.

What is Your Basis in Property?

"Basis" is another word for cost. The basis of property you buy, then, is usually its total cost to you. The cost will include the amount you paid in cash, any debt obligations you incurred, and the value of any other property or services you gave in exchange. This cost includes any sales tax you might have paid on the property, plus any shipping costs, installation costs, and testing fees. Your yearly depreciation deduction is a percentage of the basis of your property.

If you change property that you once used for personal purposes, into business use, your basis in the property for depreciation purposes, is the **lesser** of the following: (a) the fair market value of the property on the date you change it from personal use to business use, or (b) your original cost basis, plus the cost of any improvements made, minus certain tax deductions.

If you use the same property for both personal and business purposes, you can claim a depreciation deduction ONLY for the percentage of the basis that applies to the business use of the property.

Property Class

Property class establishes the recovery period for the property, that is, the number of years over which you can take the depreciation deduction. Under the General Depreciation System (GDS), property is assigned to one of 8 classes.

The established property classes under the General Depreciation System (GDS) are the following:

- 3-year property: This consists of tractor units, racehorses over two years old, and horses over 12 years old when placed in service.
- 5-year property: This consists of automobiles, taxis, buses, trucks, computers and peripheral equipment, office machinery, and any property used in research and experimentation. This property class also includes breeding and dairy cattle.
- 7-year property: This consists of office furniture and fixtures, and any property that has not been designated as belonging to another class.
- 10-year property: This consists of vessels, barges, tugs, and similar water transportation equipment, single-purpose agricultural or horticultural structures, and trees or vines bearing fruit or nuts.

- **15-year property**: This consists of depreciable improvements to land such as shrubbery, fences, roads, and bridges.
- **20-year property**: This consists of farm buildings that are not agricultural or horticultural structures.
- **27.5-year property**: This consists of residential rental property.
- **39-year property**: This consists of nonresidential real estate, including home offices.
-

The Section 179 Deduction

Under Section 179 of the Inland Revenue Code (IRC) you can benefit from a very valuable tax break, by electing to deduct all or part of the cost of certain qualifying property (up to a certain limit) in the first year you place the property in service. You could basically be allowed to take all of your total depreciation deductions up front, instead of taking them yearly over the recovery period of the property.

A taxpayer may elect to expense the cost of any section 179 property and deduct it in the year the property is placed in service. The new Tax Cuts and Jobs Act law increased the maximum deduction from $500,000 to $1 million. It also increased the phase-out threshold from $2 million to $2.5 million. For taxable years beginning after 2018, these amounts of $1 million and $2.5 million will be adjusted for inflation. The new law also expands the definition of section 179 property to allow the taxpayer to elect to include the following improvements made to nonresidential real property after the date when the property was first placed in service:

- Qualified improvement property, which means any improvement to a building's interior. However, improvements do not qualify if they are attributable to: (a) the enlargement of the building, (b) any elevator or escalator or (c) the internal structural framework of the building.
- Roofs, HVAC, fire protection systems, alarm systems and security systems.

These changes apply to property placed in service in taxable years beginning after Dec. 31, 2017.

Certain types of property do not qualify for the Section 179 deduction. These properties include:

- Property held only for the production of income.
- Rental property.
- Property used predominantly to furnish lodgings.
- Property acquired from relatives.

133

The Depreciation Limits for Auto

The new law changed depreciation limits for passenger vehicles placed in service after Dec. 31, 2017. If the taxpayer doesn't claim bonus depreciation, the greatest allowable depreciation deduction is:

- $10,000 for the first year,
- $16,000 for the second year,
- $9,600 for the third year, and
- $5,760 for each later taxable year in the recovery period.

If a taxpayer claims 100 percent bonus depreciation, the greatest allowable depreciation deduction is:

- $18,000 for the first year,
- $16,000 for the second year,
- $9,600 for the third year, and
- $5,760 for each later taxable year in the recovery period.

The new law also removes computer or peripheral equipment from the definition of listed property. This change applies to property placed in service after Dec. 31, 2017. These limits, however, do not apply to the following types of vehicles:

- Ambulances or hearses used specifically in your business.
- Taxis, transport vans, and other vehicles used specifically for transporting people or property.
- Qualified non-personal use vehicles specifically modified for business use. For example, vans without seating behind the driver, vehicles with permanent shelving installed, and vehicles with the company's name painted on the exterior.

SUVs weighting above 6,000 pounds, but no more than 14,000 pounds, qualify for expensing up to $25,000, if the vehicle is financed and placed in service during the year, and meets the other conditions.

Bonus Depreciation

The new law also increased the first-year bonus depreciation from 50% to 100% of the qualified property purchased, and expanded it to include both new and used equipment. The allowable bonus depreciation starts to decline after 2022. It falls to 80% in 2023, 60% in 2024, 40% in 2025 and 20% in 2026.

The Rules Relating to Listed Property

Listed property is any property that the IRS considers likely to be used for both business and personal purposes, and includes the following:

- Passenger automobiles weighing 6,000 pounds or less.
- Any other property used for the transportation of people (trucks, buses, boats).
- Any property used for entertainment, recreation, or amusement (cameras, DVD players, cellular phones, etc.)
- Computers that are not used exclusively at a regular business establishment.

There are special rules and record-keeping requirements for depreciating listed property. These are as follows:

- Only the business-use portion of the cost can be depreciated.
- To depreciate listed property using the GDS system, the qualified business use of the property must be more than 50% of its total use. This is called the Predominant Use Test.
- If the qualified business use of the property is 50% or less, you must depreciate using the ADS (straight-line) system and you cannot claim a Section 179 deduction.

To take a depreciation deduction for listed property, you must be able to provide supporting records and evidence to prove business use.

How to Report Disposition of Property

A disposition of property is the permanent withdrawal of property from use in a trade or business. A disposition of property can occur as a result of sale, exchange, retirement, abandonment, or destruction of the property. A disposition before the end of the recovery period is called an early disposition.

For properties depreciated under MACRS, you are allowed a depreciation deduction in the year of disposition. This deduction is usually a percentage of the MACRS deduction for that year of service. The percentage you can claim will depend on the convention you are using.

You must use IRS Form 4797 to report the sale of any property used in a business. A taxpayer who sold or transferred property used for business must fill out the form and attach it to the tax return.

You are required to include the following information on Form 4797, relating to the property disposed of:

- Description of the property.
- Date acquired.
- Date sold.
- Gross sales price.
- Cost or other basis.
- Computation of gain or loss.

(Easily available off-the-shelf software will effectively facilitate the completion of Form 4797, and calculate your gain or loss, for inclusion on your tax return.)

Amortization

In tax law, amortization refers to the cost recovery system for intangible property. To claim a deduction for amortization, the intangible property must be held either for use in a trade or business, or for the production of income.

An intangible asset is typically anything nonphysical in nature, and hard to assign an actual value to. Qualified intangible property includes noncompetitive trade agreements, goodwill, trademarks, the value of a worker's expertise, trade and franchise names, etc. Amortization is the practice of deducting the cost of an investment in a qualifying intangible asset over the estimated life of the asset, which is usually a 15-year period, regardless of the actual useful life of the asset.

Amortization vs. depreciation
Amortization is similar to the straight-line method of depreciation. It is not surprising to find depreciation and amortization being used interchangeably. This is because all methodologies for allotting amortization to each tax period are basically the same as methodologies for depreciation. In principle, however, depreciation refers to tangible assets, while amortization refers to intangible assets.

Startup costs

Investigating the potential for a new business, and actually getting it started, can be a very costly undertaking. Under the general rules for business deductions, you cannot deduct these expenses when incurred, because you can only deduct expenses for an existing trade or business. By definition, you incur your startup expenses prior to the time that your business was in existence. Tax law, however, allows you take yearly deductions for your business startup costs, through the process of amortization.

You may be able to deduct up to $5,000 of your qualifying start-up costs in the first year of operation, with a phase out of the deduction starting at $50,000.

In other words, if your start-up efforts end in the creation of an active trade or business, then on your first tax return, the amount of expenses that you can deduct will be the lesser of:

1. Your actual expenses with respect to the new business; **or**
2. $5,000, reduced by the amount by which the start-up expenditures with respect to the active trade or business exceed $50,000.

You will be able to deduct the remainder of your start-up expenditures ratably over the 180-month period beginning with the month in which the active trade or business begins.

Completing Form 4562

You are required to file a Form 4562, Depreciation and Amortization, for the first year you claim a deduction for depreciation or amortization, on any particular piece of property. You must also file Form 4562 for any year you claim a Section 179 deduction, and for every year you claim depreciation on a car, or any other type of listed property.

You must, therefore, complete Form 4562, and attach it to your return if the any of the following apply to you:

- You claim a Section 179 deduction or carryover.
- You claim a depreciation deduction for property placed in service in the current year.
- You claim a depreciation deduction on any vehicle or other listed property, regardless of the year placed in service.
- You claim a deduction for amortization of costs that begin in the current year.

You must complete and file a separate Form 4562 for each business or activity for which you are claiming a depreciation deduction. The amount on line 22 of Form 4562 must be entered on the schedule (Schedule E, or Schedule C) on which you are claiming the depreciation.

You are not required to file Form 4562 to report depreciation or amortization for non-listed property for the years after the property was placed in service.

A depreciation worksheet is provided in the instructions for Form 4562. You use this worksheet to figure your depreciation deduction, and also for record keeping.

(Easily available off-the-shelf tax software will effectively complete both Form 4562 and the depreciation worksheet, and compute the depreciation deduction, for inclusion on your tax return.)

Some Tax Planning Points

If you have not claimed depreciation for your property, or have not claimed the correct amount, the amount of depreciation that should have been claimed, even though you might not have claimed it, will be subtracted from the basis (cost) of your property when it is sold. This can have adverse effects on your finances, because what it will do in effect is to reduce the basis of your property, and hence increase any capital gain (or decrease any capital loss) that might be realized upon sale of the under-depreciated property.

To claim the special depreciation allowance for listed property, the property must be used more than 50% in a trade or business.

You can claim a depreciation deduction for computer software if: (a) it is readily available for purchase by the general public, (b) it is subject to a nonexclusive license, and (c) it is not substantially modified.

Computer software is intangible property; therefore it cannot be depreciated under MACRS. You must depreciate the cost of computer software over 36 months, using the straight-line method. The cost of computer software that does not meet the above criteria must be amortized.

Off-the-shelf computer software that is placed in service after 2002 is qualifying property for the purposes of the Section 179 deduction.

11 How to Report Your Social Security Benefits

Social Security benefits may be non-taxable or partially taxable, depending on your total income from other sources. To be more precise, your Social Security benefits may not be taxable at all, or may be taxable up to 85% of the amount. The amount that may be taxable depends basically on your total income from other sources and on your marital status.

How to Determine How Much of Your Benefits are Taxable

Generally, if Social Security benefits were your only income for the year, your benefits are not taxable, and you probably do not need to file a federal income tax return. If you received income from other sources, some of your benefits could be taxable. Your benefits, however, will not be taxed unless your modified adjusted gross income is more than the base amount (see below) established for your filing status.

You can do the following quick computation to determine whether some of your benefits may be taxable:

- First, add one-half of the total Social Security benefits you received to all your other income, including any tax-exempt interest and other exclusions from income.
- Then, compare this total to the base amount for your filing status. If the total is more than your base amount, some of your benefits may be taxable.

Your Social Security benefits include retirement, survivor, and disability benefits, and are reported to you and the IRS on Form SSA-1099.

Depending on your other income and your filing status, your benefits may not be taxable, or they may be taxable up to 85% of the benefits received. Basically, as your income increases, a greater percentage of your benefits become taxable.

Social Security benefits are not taxable if your modified adjusted gross income (AGI plus tax-exempt interest minus adjustments) plus one-half of your net Social Security benefits shown in box 5 of your Form SSA-1099 do not exceed the following base amounts:

- $25,000 if filing Single, HOH or QW.

- $25,000 if filing MFS, and lived apart from spouse for all of the tax year.
- $32,000 if filing MFJ.
- $0 if filing MFS, and did live with spouse during the year.

If your modified adjusted gross income plus one-half of your net Social Security benefits are more than the base amounts (above) you must further determine to see if they are less than the adjusted base amounts below:

- $34,000 if filing Single, HOH, or QW.
- $34,000 if filing MFS, and did not live with spouse during year.
- $44,000 if filing MFJ.
- $0 if filing MFS, and did live with spouse during the year.

If your modified AGI plus one-half of your Social Security benefits are more than the base amounts but less than the adjusted base amounts, then your taxable Social Security benefits is the SMALLER of:

- One-half of the net benefits received, or
- One-half of the excess of (modified AGI plus ½ net benefits) over the base amount.

If the sum of your modified AGI and one-half of your Social Security benefits are more than the adjusted base amounts, your taxable Social Security benefits are the SMALLER of:

- 85% of the net benefits received.
- 85% of the amount by which the sum of your modified AGI and one-half of Social Security benefits exceed the adjusted base amount, plus the smaller of: (a) 50% of Social Security benefits, (b) 50% of the amount by which the sum of AGI, nontaxable income and one-half of the Social Security benefits exceed the adjusted base amount, or (c) the adjusted base amount.

(You need not be daunted by the above, because any off-the-shelf tax software will figure the taxable amount for you.)

Note that taxable benefits should be included only in the income of the person with the legal right to receive them. Thus, a child's benefits belong to the child and should not be reported on the parent's tax return.

How to Report Tier 1 Railroad Retirement Benefits

Part of the tier 1 railroad retirement benefits is treated just as Social Security benefits for tax purposes.

- They are commonly called Social Security equivalent benefits.
- They are reported to you on Form RRB-1099.
- You use the same worksheets and rules as with Social Security benefits to determine if any part of these benefits is taxable.
- Any part that is taxable is reported on Form 1040.

Any tier 1 benefits that are not treated as Social Security equivalent benefits, plus any tier 2 benefits, and certain other railroad employee benefits, are reported on Form RRB-1099-R, and are treated as pension distributions for tax purposes.

12 How to Report Pensions, Annuities, IRAs, and other Retirement Benefits

The tax code begins to get very complex when it comes to understanding certain tax implications on retirement instruments. It is very important to be aware of the impact of tax on your retirement benefits, and in particular, the various penalties and additional taxes that you could potentially incur if you do not concur with tax law, as far as your contributions to, and distributions from your retirement instruments are concerned. The more common types of retirement benefits include pensions, annuities, and IRAs.

Defining Pensions and Annuities

In general, pensions and annuities are arrangements to provide people with an income when they are no longer earning a regular income from employment. Distributions from pensions and annuities represent the amounts of money you begin to receive from your employer upon retirement from the company. When you participate in a pension plan, you and/or your employer may make contributions to your pension, depending on the type of pension.

Whether the employer solely contributed this money, or whether you and the employer equally contributed; this factor determines the amount of taxation levied on the distributions you receive. Plans, which are paid totally by your employer, are fully taxable. Also, plans can be qualified or non-qualified.

Qualified Plans

Qualified plans allow the employer a tax deduction for contributions it makes to the plan, and employees typically do not pay taxes on plan assets until these assets are distributed; furthermore, earnings on qualified plan assets are tax deferred. Qualified pension plans allow you to contribute to your pensions on a pretax basis. Generally, contributions to a qualified retirement plan are tax-free. Tax-free contributions are contributions you can make with your pretax income. These contributions are income tax-free, regardless of whether the contributions are made by the employer or employee. Because contributions are pretax, all distributions will be fully taxable as ordinary income to the employee when the money is eventually paid out on retirement.

Non-Qualified Plans

A non-qualified deferred compensation plan or agreement simply defers the payment of a portion of the employee's compensation to a future date. The amounts are held back (deferred) while the employee is working for the company, and are paid out to the employee when he or she separates from service, becomes disabled, or dies.

In contrast to qualified plans, you have to pay tax on money you or your employer contribute to your non-qualified plan during the year you contribute it, and capital gains earned inside the plan are not tax-deferred; this means that you have to pay tax on them during the year you earned a capital gain. Contributions to these plans are not tax-deductible, but funds do grow tax-deferred and will be taxed when distributions are made upon retirement.

Contributions

During your working life you can make elective deferrals to a qualified retirement plan if your employer operates such a plan. This means that you can choose to have part of your compensation (subject to annual limits) contributed by your employer to a retirement fund. This contribution is not included in your wages, and is not subject to income tax at the time it is made.

Distributions

At some time in the future you will begin to take distributions from the plan, and these distributions will be taxable in the year you receive them. The financial institution reports your distributions to you and the IRS on Form 1099-R. The distribution code defines the type of distribution, and this is reported in box 7 of Form 1099-R.

Distributions from pensions and annuities are fully taxable if you did not pay any part of the cost of your employee pension or annuity with after-tax money, and/or you deferred part of your pay while you worked. If you made after-tax contributions to the cost of the plan, your pensions and annuities will be partially taxable, depending on the amount of after-tax contributions you made.

The Simplified Method

If you made after-tax contributions to your pension or annuity plan, part of your pension or annuity payments will be tax-free. You must figure this tax-free part when the payments first begin. The tax-free amount remains the same each year, even if the amount of the payment changes. The pension or annuity sponsor may compute the tax-free amount for you and report it in

Box 5 of the 1099-R information statement that you receive. However, in some cases, you'll have to compute it yourself. You generally figure the tax free and taxable parts of pension or annuity payments by using the Simplified Method worksheet, in the Form 1040 instructions.

If you began receiving distributions after November 18, 1996, and they are from a qualified retirement plan payable over your life, or over the life of a beneficiary, you are required to use the Simplified Method to figure the taxable amount for the year. What the Simplified Method worksheet does is to exclude the nontaxable pension, until your after-tax cost in the pension or annuity is recovered. After your after-tax cost is recovered, the entire pension is taxable.

(Most off-the-shelf software will facilitate the completion on the Simplified Method worksheet, and include the taxable portion of your pension/annuity on your tax return.)

Defining Traditional IRAs

An IRA (individual retirement arrangement) is a personal savings plan, which allows you to set aside money for retirement, while offering you some tax advantages. An IRA is a trust or custodial account set up in the U.S. for the exclusive benefit of the taxpayer, or the taxpayer's beneficiaries. The trustee or custodian must be a bank, a federally insured credit union, a savings and loans association, or an entity approved by the IRS to act as trustee or custodian.

You may be able to claim a tax deduction for some or all of the contributions you make to a traditional IRA. You may also be eligible for a tax credit equal to a percentage of your contribution. Amounts in your traditional IRA, including earnings, generally are not taxed until they are eventually distributed to you.

The Rules Relating to Traditional IRAs

An IRA is an investing tool used by individuals to earn and earmark funds for retirement savings. Generally, the following rules apply to traditional IRAs:

- The maximum contribution you can make to a traditional IRA each year is $5,500 ($6,500 if you are 50 or older).
- You cannot contribute to a traditional IRA if you are over age 70 ½.You must begin to take distributions from your traditional IRAs by April 1 of the year following the calendar year in which you reach the age of 70 ½.

- You can make a contribution to your IRA at any time before the due date of your tax return. (For example, for tax year 2018, you may make contributions up to April 15, 2019).
- The amounts that you earn on your contributions are not taxable until they are eventually withdrawn.
- There are additional taxes and penalties for excess contributions, early withdrawals, and excess accumulations (see below).
- You may also establish a traditional IRA for your spouse, but you must file MFJ (see below).
- The proceeds from inherited IRAs are generally fully taxable, unless the deceased made some nondeductible contributions.
- The amount you invest in the IRA must be fully vested. This means that you must have a non-forfeitable right to the amount invested at all times.
- The contributions must be in cash, except that rollover contributions can be property other than cash.
- You cannot use money in the account to buy a life insurance policy.

Reporting Distributions

One of the provisions of an individual retirement account is that you must eventually begin taking money (distributions) out of the account. Distributions, then, are amounts that you receive from your retirement accounts. When you receive distributions from your traditional IRA, these amounts may be fully or partly taxable. This all depends on whether your IRA includes any nondeductible (after-tax) contributions.

If you made only deductible contributions to your traditional IRA, meaning that you did not contribute any after-tax money, this means that you will have no basis (after-tax contribution) in the IRA, and all distributions will be fully taxable when received.

Distributions are reported to you on Form 1099-R, with the distribution code shown in box 7, and the IRA box checked.

If you made nondeductible (after-tax) contributions, or rolled over any after-tax amounts to any of your traditional IRAs, you would have a cost basis (investment in the contract) equal to the amount of those contributions. These nondeductible (after-tax) contributions are not taxed when they are distributed to you, because you have already paid tax on these amounts; these amounts are a return of your investment in the IRA. Only the part of the distribution that represents nondeductible contributions and rolled over after-tax amounts is tax free.

If nondeductible contributions have been made, or after-tax amounts have been rolled over to your IRA, your distributions will consist on one part of your nondeductible contributions (which are not taxable), and on the other part of your deductible contributions and your earnings (which are taxable). Until your entire basis in the plan has been distributed, each distribution will be partly nontaxable, and partly taxable.

You must complete Form 8606, Nondeductible IRAs, and attach it to your return, if you received a distribution from a traditional IRA, and have made nondeductible contributions, or rolled over after-tax amounts to any of your traditional IRAs. This form also serves a record keeping purpose, and will enable you to figure the nontaxable distributions for 2018, and your total nondeductible IRA contributions for earlier years.

Required Minimum Distributions (RMDs)

You are required to begin withdrawing a minimum amount from your IRA account no later than April 1 of the year after you reach age 70½. (or, for most employer plan participants, after you retire). This amount is referred to as the Required Minimum Distributions. This rule exists so that the government will eventually begin to collect taxes on the tax-deferred account. If you withdraw less than the required minimum amount, you will be subject to a federal penalty, which is an excise tax equal to 50% of the amount that should have been withdrawn.

Making Contributions

If you are under age 70 ½ you can contribute each year to a traditional IRA. If neither you nor your spouse participates in a retirement plan at work, your contributions are fully tax deductible. However, if you are covered by a qualified retirement plan at work, your deduction for traditional IRA contributions is reduced according to your income and tax filing status.

The maximum contribution you can make to a traditional IRA is $5,500 ($6,500, if you are over 50). You contribution however, cannot exceed your total compensation (earned income) for the year. Contributions can be made up to the due date of filing your return (normally April 15).

Compensation, in the context of contributing to an IRA includes the following:

- Salaries and wages.
- Commissions.
- Self-employment income.
- Alimony and separate maintenance payments.
- Nontaxable combat pay.

The requirement is that you must have earned income for the year. This means that you must have earned money during the year, and your contributions will have to come from this money that you earned.

Note that when figuring total compensation for IRA contributions, any self-employment loss you incurred should not be subtracted from salaries and wages received.

Compensation in the context of contribution to a traditional IRA does not include the following:

- Earnings and profits from property, such as rental income, interest income, and dividend income.
- Pension or annuity income.
- Deferred income received (compensation payments postponed from a past year).
- Income from a partnership for which you provide no services that are a material income-producing factor.
- Any amounts excluded from income, such as foreign earned income and housing costs.

- If you are filing MFJ, you and your spouse can each contribute to an IRA, but the combined contribution cannot exceed $11,000 (12,000 if one is 50 or over, or $13,000 if both of you are 50 and over). Again, your combined contribution cannot exceed you and your spouse's total taxable compensation. You can contribute to a spousal IRA until reaching age 70 ½.

Deductibility of Contributions to Tradition IRAs

When you contribute to a traditional IRA, part or all of your contributions may be tax deductible, and these deductions are claimed as an adjustment to income on Schedule 1, line 28. Contributions to a traditional IRA might be fully deductible, partially deductible, or not deductible at all, depending on factors such as your age, your modified adjusted gross income, marital status, and whether you, or your spouse, are covered by a retirement plan through your employer. Your modified AGI must be figured without taking into account any of following: (a) the IRA deduction, (b) student loan interest deduction, and (c) tuition and fees deduction.

Not covered by an employer plan
If you are not covered by an employer retirement plan, you can take a full deduction on your allowed contribution.

Covered by an employer plan

147

If you are covered by an employer retirement plan, the amount of the contribution that can be deducted may be phased out, or eliminated entirely, depending on your modified AGI and your filing status. The phase-out ranges are as follows:

- Single or HOH – begins to phase out at $63,000: eliminated at $74,000.
- MFJ or QW – begins to phase out at $103,000: eliminated at $123,000.
- MFS – begins to phase out at $0: eliminated at $10,000.

Spouse covered by an employer plan
If you are not covered by an employer retirement plan, but your spouse is, the amount of your deduction may be reduced, or eliminated entirely, depending on your modified AGI and filing status. The phase-out ranges are as follows:

- MFJ – begins to phase out at $189,000: eliminated at $199,000.
- MFS – begins to phase out at $0: eliminated at $10,000.

(Any off-the-shelf tax software will effectively calculate your allowable deduction, for inclusion in your tax return.)

Nondeductible IRA contributions

If you made non-deductible contributions to your IRA, it is to your benefit that you report these contributions on Form 8606. This is to establish a basis in your IRA. If Form 8606 is not filed, the nondeductible contribution will be treated as if it were deductible, and all distributions from the IRA will be taxed, unless you can otherwise show that nondeductible contributions were made.

Prohibited Transactions

There are certain transactions concerning an IRA, which the IRS specifically prohibits. Generally, a prohibited transaction is any improper use of an IRA account or annuity by the IRA owner, his or her beneficiary, or any disqualified person. Disqualified persons include the IRA owner's fiduciary and members of his or her family (spouse, ancestor, lineal descendant, and any spouse of a lineal descendant). The following are examples of prohibited transactions with a traditional IRA:

- Borrowing money from it.
- Selling property to it.
- Receiving unreasonable compensation for managing it.
- Using it as security for a loan.

- Buying property for personal use (present or future) with IRA funds.

There is a 15% excise tax on the amount of the prohibited transaction, and a 100% additional tax if the transaction is not corrected. If you engage in a prohibited transaction, your IRA will cease to be a qualified IRA, and you must include the fair market value of the IRA assets as income in your tax return for that year. You may also have to pay the additional 10% tax on premature distribution.

Additional Taxes for Violating Qualified Plans

Qualified plans include IRAs and other tax-favored (tax-deferred) accounts. To discourage the use of retirement funds for purposes other than normal retirement, the law imposes additional taxes if you violate the rules relating to early distributions of those funds, and on failures to withdraw the funds timely. Violations of qualified plans generally include: (a) premature distributions, (b) excess contributions, and (c) excess accumulations.

You must use Form 5329, Additional Taxes on Qualified Plans (Including IRAs) and Other Tax-Favored Accounts, to figure and report any additional taxes that result from these violations. Even if you do not have to file a tax return, you must send the IRS a completed Form 5329.

Tax on Premature Distributions (Early Withdrawals)

As a general rule, a premature distribution is any money you take out of your retirement plan before you reach age 59 ½. As a deterrent to taxpayers taking premature distributions, tax law imposes an <u>additional</u> tax of 10% on certain early distributions taken from your retirement funds. This is to ensure that your retirement plan is used for the purpose it was established.

When there is a premature (early) distribution, the following rules will apply:

- The financial institution will show the appropriate distribution code (code1) in box 7 of Form 1099-R.
- You will be liable for an additional tax of 10% on the part of the distribution that you will have to include in your gross income.
- The additional 10% tax does not apply to the nontaxable part of the distribution.
- You may have to file Form 5329 if you owe any additional tax on the distribution.

Tax law allows a number of exceptions to the 10% additional tax rule. This means that you would not be liable for the additional 10% tax on the early distribution if any of the conditions stated below exist:

- Any amounts withdrawn from your retirement account are rolled over into another qualified plan within 60 days.
- You received your distributions in the form of an annuity (code 2 on 1099-R). This means that you received distributions as part of a series of substantially equal periodic payments over your life expectancy, or the joint life expectancy of you and your beneficiary.
- You become totally and permanently disabled (code 3 on 1099-R).
- You are the beneficiary of a deceased IRA owner (code 4 on 1099-R).
- You receive distributions to the extent of un-reimbursed deductible medical expenses that exceed 7.5% of your adjusted gross income (code 5 on 1099-R).
- You received unemployment that was includible in income, and had an IRA distribution that was used for health insurance (code 7 on 1099-R).
- You received IRA distributions to pay for qualified higher education expenses (code 8 of 1099-R). These are not subject to the additional tax as long as they do not exceed the qualified higher education expenses. You must complete form 5329, listing your total distribution from your IRA and the amount that was used for higher education expenses. Next to Line 2, write the code "08" to signify that you used the money for higher education expenses.
- You used up to $10,000 of your IRA distribution to buy, build, or rebuild your first home, and did not own a home in the previous two years ending on the date of acquisition of your home (code 9 on 1099-R).
- You received distributions after you separated from service after reaching 55 years of age (employer plans only).
- The distribution is due to an IRS levy on the qualified plan.
- If distribution code 2, 3, or 4 is shown in box 7 of Form 1099-R, and you qualify for an exemption to the 10% tax, you do not have to file Form 5329. You must file Form 5329 if no code is shown in box 7, or code 1 is shown and you meet one of the exceptions.

Tax on Excess Contributions

An excess contribution occurs when you put more money into your individual retirement account (IRA) than the law allows. You would have made an excess contribution if the amount contributed to your traditional IRA exceeds the amount that you are allowed to contribute. The amount you are allowed to contribute is the smaller of:

- $5,500 ($6,500, if you are 50 or older), or
- Your taxable compensation for the year.

The taxable compensation limit applies whether the contributions are deductible or nondeductible. Note that any contributions you make to your plan for the year you reach 70 ½ or any later years are also considered excess contributions.

If you do not withdraw your excess contributions by the due date of your tax return (including extensions) you will be subject to a 6% excise tax.

You will not be subject to the 6% tax if the excess contributions made during a tax year is withdrawn, and any interest or other income earned on the excess contribution is also withdrawn by the due date of the return (including extensions). Note however, that the interest and other income withdrawn may be subject to the additional 10% tax on early distributions.

Tax on Excess Accumulations

Excess accumulations occur when the owner or the beneficiary of a retirement account fails to take the annual required minimum distribution (RMD) that he/she is required to take from the retirement account.

The rules are as follows:

- Tax law mandates that you must begin taking distributions from your retirement account by April 1 of the year following the year you reach 70 ½.
- If you do not take the required minimum distribution, or if the distributions you take are less than the required minimum amount, you may have to pay a 50% excise tax on the amount that was not taken out of the account as required.

You can figure your required minimum distribution for each year by dividing the IRA account balance by the applicable life expectancy.

If the excess accumulation is due to reasonable error, and if the account holder or beneficiary has taken, or are taking steps to remedy the insufficient distribution, the tax may be excused if the IRA owner or beneficiary does the following:

- File IRS Form 5329 with or without Form 1040.
- Attach a letter of explanation and request a waiver.

If the IRS approves the request, the excess accumulations tax will be waived. It is imperative that you follow the instructions for Form 5329 to the letter.

IRA Rollovers

Generally, an IRA rollover is a tax-free transfer of cash or other assets from one qualified retirement plan to another qualified retirement plan. A rollover is thus nothing but a movement of funds from one retirement plan into another. The transfer can be made either by means of a direct transfer or by way of check. This transfer of funds from one plan to the second retirement plan is called a "rollover contribution." The most common type of IRA rollover occurs when an employee leaves a company and wants to take their retirement money with them, instead of leaving it in their old employer's plan.

A rollover has to be reported to the IRS, and is therefore subject to monitoring and supervision by the IRS. The following rules apply to rollovers:

- To avoid any tax liability, you must complete the rollover by the 60th day following the day you receive the funds. You are therefore not liable for taxes on any amounts you rollover within the 60 day limit.
- If you have the distribution paid directly to you, the plan administrator must withhold income tax of 20% from the taxable distribution. With this in mind, it will be more advantageous, therefore, if you do a direct rollover rather than having the check paid to you, because in a direct rollover the plan administrator will not withhold taxes from your distribution.

Defining Roth IRAs

A Roth IRA is an individual retirement plan, which allows taxpayers, subject to certain income limits, to save for retirement while allowing the savings to grow tax-free. With Roth IRAs, contributions are not tax deductible, but withdrawals from the plan, subject to certain rules, are not taxed at all. Roth IRAs are subject to the same rules that apply to traditional IRAs, except that contributions are nondeductible, and qualified distributions are tax-free.

Contributions to Roth IRAs

The following rules apply for making contributions to a Roth IRA:

- You cannot deduct contributions you make to a Roth IRA.
- You can contribute to a Roth IRA regardless of your age.
- Like traditional IRAs, the maximum contribution you can make to a Roth IRA is the lesser of: (a) $5,500 ($6,500 if age 50 or over), or (b) your taxable compensation.
- If you contribute to both Roth IRAs and traditional IRAs, your contribution limit for Roth IRAs must be reduced by all contributions for the year to your traditional IRAs.

- If you make excess contributions to a Roth IRA, you will be subject to a 6% excise tax.

Distributions from Roth IRAs

The tax treatment of a Roth IRA distribution depends on whether the distribution is qualified. Qualified distributions from Roth IRAs are tax and penalty free, but nonqualified distributions may be subjected to tax and an early distribution penalty.

A qualified distribution is any distribution from a Roth IRA that is taken 5 years after the last taxable year for which a contribution was made. To be completely tax-free, however, the distribution must meet at least one of the following requirements:

- It is made on or after you reach age 59 ½.
- It is made because you became disabled.
- It is made to a beneficiary or to the taxpayer's estate after death.
- It is used to buy, build, or rebuild a first home (up to a $10,000 lifetime limit).

As with traditional IRAs, any non-qualifying distributions from a Roth IRA are subject to a 10% additional tax.

Distributions from a Roth IRA are reported to you on Form 1099-R with "J", "Q" or "T" coded in box 7.

The minimum distribution rules that apply to traditional IRAs do not apply to Roth IRAs, therefore you can leave amounts in your Roth IRA account for as long as you live.

Converting a Traditional IRA to a Roth IRA

You can convert amounts from a traditional IRA, SEP, or SIMPLE IRA into a Roth IRA, but you will have to pay income tax on the amounts converted. The amount that is converted is added to your income and is fully taxable. There is no 10% early withdrawal penalty if the funds are moved from the traditional IRA to the Roth IRA within the 60-day window. A conversion is reported as code 2 in box 2 of Form 1099-R. You can now convert a traditional IRA to a Roth IRA regardless of income.

There are three different Roth IRA conversion methods you can use. These are as follows:

(a) Rollover - You can receive a distribution from a traditional IRA, 401k, or other qualified retirement plan and roll it over (contribute it) to your Roth IRA within 60 days of receiving the distribution.

(b) Trustee-to-Trustee Transfer - You can direct the trustee of your current retirement account to transfer funds to the trustee of your Roth IRA account.

(c) Same Trustee Transfer - If the retirement account that you plan to convert is overseen by the same trustee who oversees your Roth IRA, then you can direct the trustee to simply transfer funds from the first account to your Roth IRA. You also have the option to simply re-designate your current account as a Roth IRA, rather than open a new account and/or issue a new contract.

If you inherited a traditional IRA from someone other than a spouse, you cannot convert the traditional IRA into a Roth IRA.

If you started taking equal periodic distributions from a traditional IRA, you can convert the amounts in the traditional IRA to a Roth IRA and then continue the periodic payments. The 10% tax on early distributions will not apply.

Making Contributions to Both Roth IRAs and Traditional IRAs

You can contribute to both Roth IRAs and traditional IRAs in the same year, but the contribution limit for Roth IRAs is the **lesser** of:

- The maximum contribution limit ($5,500 or $6,500 if over 50) reduced by all contributions (other than employer contributions under a SEP or SIMPLE IRA plan) for the year, to all IRAs other than Roth IRAs, or
- The maximum contribution, as phased out, because modified AGI is above a certain amount (see below).

For tax year 2018, your Roth IRA contribution limit is reduced (phased out) in the following situations:

- Single, HOH or MFS and did not live with spouse at any time during the year – begins to phase out at $120,000: eliminated at $135,000.
- MFJ or QW – begins to phase out at $189,000: eliminated at $199,000.
- MFS – begins to phase out at $0: eliminated at $10,000.

Reporting Disability Income

If you retired on disability, you must include in your taxable income any disability pension you receive under a plan that is paid for by your employer. You must report your taxable disability payments as wages until you reach minimum retirement age. Minimum retirement age generally is the age at which you can first receive a pension or annuity if you are not disabled. The following rules apply to reporting disability income:

- Your employer will report your disability income to you either on Form W-2 or Form 1099-R.
- If reported on Form 1099-R, box 2a will show the taxable amount, and box 7 will show the code number 3.
- You must report all taxable disability income until you reach minimum retirement age.
-
- Because the IRS considers disability retirement benefits as earned income <u>until</u> you reach minimum retirement age, you can use this income to qualify for the earned income credit, if all the other conditions are met.

How to Claim the Retirement Savings Contribution Credit (Saver's Credit)

You may be eligible for a tax credit if you make eligible contributions to an employer-sponsored retirement plan or to an individual retirement arrangement.
You're eligible for this credit if you are:

- Age 18 or older.
- Not a full-time student.
- Not claimed as a dependent on another person's return.

The maximum you could receive in a given year is $1,000 on a retirement contribution of $2,000 (double those numbers if married and filing jointly).

- The AGI (adjusted gross income) limit for the saver's credit is:
- $31,500 for single filers and married individuals filing separately
- $47,250 for heads of household
- $63,000 for married couples filing jointly

The Saver's Credit can be taken for your contributions to a traditional or Roth IRA; your 401(k), SIMPLE IRA, SARSEP, 403(b), 501(c)(18) or governmental 457(b) plan; and your voluntary after-tax employee contributions to your qualified retirement and 403(b) plans.

Rollover contributions aren't eligible for the Saver's Credit. Also, your eligible contributions may be reduced by any recent distributions you received from a retirement plan or IRA. You claim this credit by completing Form 8880.

(Any off-the shelf tax software will effectively complete Form 8880, and compute the credit for inclusion on your tax return.)

13 Reporting Capital Gains and Losses

A capital gain is a profit that results from the sale of capital assets, such as stocks, bonds, or real estate. It is the amount by which what you sold the asset for exceeds the asset's cost to you. Conversely, a capital loss arises if the proceeds from the sale of a capital asset are less than the asset's cost. The objective of this chapter is to give you an understanding of how to calculate your capital gains or losses, and especially how to treat a gain on the sale of your private residence. A great deal of emphasis is also placed on the basis (cost) of your property, which figures predominantly in the calculation of your capital gains or losses.

Definition of Capital Assets

Almost everything you own and use for personal or investment purposes is a capital asset. When you sell a capital asset, the difference between the amount you sell it for, and your basis (what you paid for it) is a capital gain or a capital loss. You must report all capital gains as income, but you may deduct capital losses only on investment property, not on property held for personal use.

Capital assets include the following:

- Stocks and bonds.
- A home owned and occupied by you and your family.
- Household furnishings.
- Your personal car used for pleasure and commuting.
- Gems and jewelry.
- Coin and stamp collections.
- Gold, silver, and other metals.
- Timber grown on your property.

The following are not capital assets:

- Property held for resale to customers, or property that will become part of merchandise for sale to customers.
- Depreciable property used in a trade or business.
- Real property used in a trade or business.
- Supplies of a type regularly used or consumed in the ordinary course of a trade or business.

- A copyright, a literary, musical, or artistic composition, or a letter or memorandum.

Since these items are not capital assets, gains or losses arising from the sale of these items will not be reported as capital gains or losses, but will be reported on other forms or schedules.

Defining Your Basis in Property

Your basis in property you dispose of is a very important number in your capital gains calculations, and is usually its cost to you (how much you actually paid for the property). Your basis in property, therefore, is the amount of your investment in the property, for tax purposes.

Your original basis (cost), however, can be subject to adjustments; for example, improvements to the property will increase your basis, whereas depreciation or casualty losses will decrease your basis. The original cost of property is the amount you pay for it in cash, debt obligations, or other property or services.

It is very important to be able to accurately determine the basis of your property, because your basis is used to figure the amounts for depreciation, amortization, depletion, charitable gifts, and casualty loses, all of which can have an impact on the computation of your capital gains or losses, upon the sale or other disposition of your property.

Generally, the higher the basis of your property, the less the gain that is reported on sale; and the lower the basis of your property, the higher will be the gain reported on the sale. You should therefore keep proper records, to ensure that the basis of your property can be accurately determined.

The Cost Basis

The cost basis of property is usually its original purchase price. In addition to the price you paid for the property, basis also includes the following: sales tax, freight charges, installation and testing charges, excise taxes, legal fees, revenue stamps, recording fees, and real estate taxes (if these are assumed for the seller). The basis of stocks and bonds is the purchase price, plus any costs of purchase or sale, such as commissions, recording and transfer fees, etc. You may use the average basis for mutual fund shares, if they are acquired at different times and prices, and are left on deposit in the account kept by the agent.

If you purchase real property (real estate), certain fees and other expenses are treated as a part of the basis. These include: taxes you agree to pay that were owed by the seller, certain settlement fees, closing costs, and expenses you pay for construction of non-business property. You must allocate the cost of real property, between land and improvements (buildings, etc.), to figure your basis for depreciation, because land is not depreciable property.

The Adjusted Basis

The adjusted basis of property is the net cost of the property after adjusting for various tax-related items. To be more specific, adjusted basis (or adjusted tax basis) refers to the original cost or other basis of property, reduced by depreciation deductions, and increased by capital expenditures relating to improvements to the property.

In computing adjusted basis, to the original purchase price of the property, add the following:

- Cost of improvements.
- Legal fees related to the purchase or use of the asset.
- Selling costs.

Reduce the above by the following:

- Accumulated depreciation.
- Losses (casualty or theft).
- Other tax-related costs and losses.

The end result of this computation is your adjusted basis

Other Basis

When cost or adjusted basis cannot be used to measure your basis in property, other methods must be used to determine your basis for tax purposes. In these situations, the main factor in determining your basis is how you actually acquired the property, and in most cases, the fair market value (FMV) of the property is used as the basis.

For example, if you received property for services you rendered, you must include the fair market value (FMV) of the property you received, in your taxable income. The amount that you include in your taxable income will now become the basis for the property you received. Also, if you inherited the property from a decedent, the basis in the property is generally the FMV at the time of the death of the person you inherited the property from.

If you dispose of property, which you had received as a gift, there are two scenarios to consider in determining which basis you should use in figuring the capital gain or loss on such property:

- If at the time you received the gift, the FMV of the property was MORE than the donor's basis, you must use the donor's basis to figure your gain or loss.
- If at the time you received the gift, the FMV of the property was LESS than the donor's basis: (a) if there is a gain on sale, you must use the donor's basis as your basis, (b) if there is a loss on the sale, you must use the FMV as your basis.

If you changed personal-use property into business or rental use property, the basis for depreciation is the **lesser** of: (a) the fair market value (FMV) of the property on the date of change, or (b) the adjusted basis on the date of change.

When You Sell Property

When you sell or trade a capital asset, a taxable gain (or loss) may result from the transaction. A sale is a transfer of your property to another party in return for money, a mortgage, a note, or other promise to pay money. A trade is a transfer of property in exchange for other property or services, and may be taxed in the same way as a sale.

Any income produced as a result of the sale of a capital asset must be reported on your income tax return as a capital gain. The amount of the capital gain you will report depends on these three factors: (a) how long you have held the asset for, (b) your basis in the asset, and (c) how much you sold the asset for.

How to Figure Capital Gains and Losses

You figure a capital gain or loss on a sale or trade by comparing the amount you received from the sale or trade with the adjusted basis of the property.

- If the amount you receive from the sale is more than the adjusted basis of the property, the result is a capital gain.
- If the amount you receive from the sale is less than the adjusted basis of the property, the result is a capital loss.

The Capital Gains Tax rate

A capital gain is usually taxed at a lower rate than ordinary income. The rates for tax year 2018 are as follows:

Tax rate	Single	MFJ	HOH
0%	$0 to $38,600	$0 to $77,200	$0 to $51,700
15%	$38,601 - $425,800	$77,201 to $479,000	$51,701 to $452,400
20%	$425,801 and up	$479,001 and up	$452,401 and up

Sales and Exchanges between Related Persons

For sales and exchanges between related persons, any gain realized may be taxed as ordinary income, even if the property is a capital asset. Related parties include members of your family, including your spouse, siblings or half-siblings, ancestors, or descendants

Related parties also include a partnership or corporation in which you control more than 50 percent of the interests, and a tax-exempt or charitable organization controlled by you or a member of your family. Also, you cannot deduct a loss incurred on the sale of property to a related party, but if the property is later sold or traded by the related party at a gain, that party can reduce that gain, by the amount of the loss that was previously disallowed to you.

How to Report Capital Gains and Losses

You must report all your capital gains and losses on Schedule D, Capital Gains and Losses, but first, you must report all capital transactions on Form 8949, Sales and Other Disposition of Capital Assets. All capital transactions must first be listed on the new Form 8949, and the subtotals from this form carried over to Schedule D, where the gain or loss for the year is calculated in aggregate.

The IRS requires that each transaction reported on Form 8949, should fall into one of these three categories:

- Transactions reported to you on Form 1099-B, on which the broker reports the cost basis of the assets sold.
- Transactions reported to you on Form 1099-B, on which the broker does not report the cost basis of the assets sold.
- Transactions that are not reported on a Form 1099-B.

A separate Form 8949 is required for each category identified above. Schedule D is now simply a summary of all capital transactions. Form 8949 must be included with Schedule D for reporting your investment activity for the year.

Defining the Holding Period

How you report a capital gain or loss depends on how long you held the asset before selling or exchanging it. This is referred to as the holding period. The holding period of an asset is of significant importance, in that it determines whether the gain or loss on disposition of the asset is considered a short-term or long-term gain or loss.

(a) Short-term holding period: If the asset is held for one year or less, the holding period is short-term, and the gain or loss is considered short-term. Short-term capital gains are taxed at the <u>higher</u> ordinary income tax rates.

(b) Long-term holding period: If the asset is held for more than one year, the holding period is long-term, and the gain or loss is considered long-term. Long-term capital gains are taxed at the favorable, discounted capital gains tax rates, which will be either zero percent, or the maximum 23.8% of the gain, depending on your marginal tax bracket.

For certain types of property, the rules for determining the holding period are established by tax law. These types of property are as follows:

- Inherited property: Property that you inherit is always considered long-term property, regardless of how long you held the property.
- Stocks and bonds bought on a securities market: Your holding period starts on the day after the trading date you bought the security, and ends on the trading date you sold the security.
- U.S. Treasury notes and bonds: If they are bought at an auction, your holding period begins on the day after notification of the bid acceptance. If they are bought through subscription, the holding period begins on the day after the subscription is submitted.
- Non-taxable exchanges: Your holding period begins on the date after you acquired the **old** property that you exchanged for the new one.
- Gifts: There are two scenarios with gifts. (a) If your basis is figured using the donor's adjusted basis, your holding period starts on the same day the donor's holding period began. (b) If your basis is figured using fair market value (FMV), your holding period starts on the day after receiving the gift.
- Real property you bought: Your holding period starts the day after you received the title for the property.
- Real property you repossessed: Your holding period begins on the date you originally received the title to the property, but does not include the time between the original sale and date of repossession.

You report the summary of your short-term gains or losses on Part I of Schedule D, and report the summary of your long-term gains or losses on Part II of Schedule D. Net short-term capital gain or loss is reported on line 7 of Schedule D; net long-term capital gain or loss is reported on line 15 on Schedule D.

Installment Sales

An installment sale occurs when you sell property at a gain, but in which you receive the sales price in installments, with at least one payment being received after the tax year in which the sale occurs.

For property sold on an installment basis, if it was long-term property in the year of sale, it stays long-term throughout the installment arrangement, and you pay tax at the lower capital gains rate. If it was short-term property in the year of sale, it remains short-term throughout the installment arrangement, and you pay tax at the normal income tax rate.

If your sale results in a loss, you cannot use the installment method. If the loss is on an installment sale of business or investment property, you can deduct it only in the tax year of sale.

Nonbusiness Bad Debts

If someone owes you money that you cannot collect, you may have a bad debt, and you may be eligible for a tax deduction. There are two kinds of bad debts - - business and nonbusiness. Generally, a business bad debt is one that comes from operating your trade or business, and these are deducted against business income. Any bad debt that is not related to the operation of a business is a nonbusiness bad debt.

Nonbusiness bad debts are considered short-term capital losses, and are deducted on Part 1 of Schedule D.

To prove a nonbusiness bad debt, you must show that there was an intention at the time of the transaction, to make a loan and not a gift. If you lend money to a relative or friend with the understanding that it may not be repaid, it is considered a gift and not a loan, and does not qualify to be classified as a nonbusiness bad debt.

How to Report Qualified Dividends and Capital Gain Distributions

These are certain types of dividends and distributions that are taxed at capital gains rates, instead of the higher income tax rates. These are as follows:

Qualified dividends: A qualified dividend is a dividend paid by a stock that meets certain requirements that allow it to be taxed at a lower rate, than at an individual's normal income tax rate. They are therefore a type of dividend to which capital gains tax rates apply, instead of the higher income tax rates.

Capital gain distributions: These are distributions that are paid to a mutual fund's shareholders out of the capital gains of the company's investment portfolio. A capital gain distribution is taxed as a long-term capital gain. This holds true even for shareholders who have held the mutual fund shares for less than a year. Generally, this means that favorable capital gains rates will apply; you are likely to pay less tax on this type of dividend than on an ordinary dividend. You report capital gain distributions on line 13 on Schedule D.

Figuring Your Capital Gains Tax

If you had capital gains, or received qualified dividends or capital gain distributions during the year, you cannot go directly to the tax tables to figure your tax. Rather, you figure your tax by completing the Qualified Dividends and Capital Gain Tax Worksheet. You must use this worksheet to figure the tax on your total income, (that is, your other taxable income plus your capital gains). You must use this worksheet, because capital gains are taxed at a different (lower) rate than ordinary income, and the tax tables by themselves, would not suffice in calculating the tax.

Capital Loss Limits and Carryover

A capital loss occurs when you sell an asset for less than its cost, or basis. A capital loss is essentially the difference between net proceeds received from the sale of an asset, and the cost of the asset, where the amount received is less than the cost. Capital losses are usually offset against capital gains, but if your capital losses exceed your capital gains, you may be able to claim a capital loss deduction on your tax return.

The IRS, however, places a limit on the amount of capital losses you can deduct. The maximum amount you are allowed to deduct for a capital loss each year is $3,000. If you are filing MFS, this maximum amount is reduced to $1,500.

You may deduct capital losses only on investment property; not on property held for personal use. Therefore, any loss on personal use property such as

164

your main homes and personal automobiles are not considered a capital loss deduction. Deductible capital losses are reported on Schedule D.

In deducting your capital losses, the following rules apply:

- You report a net capital loss on Form 1040, and you must enclose it in parentheses.
- If your net capital loss is more than the yearly limit for capital loss deductions, you can carry over the unused part to later years, until it is completely used up.
- You must use the Capital Loss Carryover Worksheet to figure the loss that can be deducted.

(Any off-the-shelf tax software will effectively include your capital loss deduction on your tax return, and compute the amount of any carry-over to future years.)

The Rules Relating to Stock Transactions

If you sold stocks and bonds during the year, you should receive a Form 1099-B from your stockbrokers. The stockbroker reports the sales price in box 2 of Form 1099-B, and checks the appropriate square, to indicate whether they reported gross or net proceeds to the IRS. The IRs requires mutual fund companies and brokerage firms to disclose on Form 1099-B, the cost basis of mutual funds and stocks sold, along with the sales prices.

There are a number of rules and regulations relating to transactions in stocks and bonds. These are as follows:

- If at the time of sale, you cannot identify the specific block from which the stocks are sold, you must treat the shares sold as coming from the earliest block.
- New stock acquired in a tax-free stock dividend (stock split) has the same holding period as the original stock owned.
- A return of capital (also known as a capital dividend) is a return of your investment; it is a distribution that is not from the corporation's earnings and profits. Consequently, such a distribution is not taxable, but it reduces the basis of the existing stock. Distributions in excess of the basis of the stock, however, are taxed as a capital gain.
- No gain or loss is recognized from the conversion of bonds into stock, or the conversion of preferred stock into common stock, in the same corporation.
- A loss on a wash sale is not deductible; the disallowed loss is added to the basis of the new stock purchased. A wash sale occurs when you sell or trade stock or securities at a loss, and within 30 days before or after the sale, you buy substantially identical stock or securities.

- Securities becoming worthless during the year are treated as though they were sold on the last day of the year.
- You report stock transactions in Parts 1 and II of Schedule D, dividing them between short-term and long-term.

The Exclusion of Gain on Sale of a Principal Residence

If certain conditions are met, you may qualify to exclude from taxable income, all or part of any gain from the sale of your main home. Your main home is where you live most of the time, and can be any of the following: house, houseboat, mobile home, trailer, cooperative apartment, or condo.

Reporting the Sale

Generally, you are not required to report the sale of your main home on your tax return, unless some of the gain from the sale is taxable. You will only be required to report the sale of your main home, if the any of following conditions apply:

- You have a gain from the sale of your home, and do not qualify to exclude all of it.
- You have a gain from the sale of your home, but choose not to exclude it.

Some people may however, still want to report the sale to the IRS. If you received a **Form 1099-S**, **Proceeds from Real Estate Transactions**, and all of your gain from the sale is excludable, you can show the sale transaction, and the exclusion of the gain, on your tax return, so that the IRS will see that the gain on the sale of your home was properly excluded. Keep in mind, however, that this property cannot be a rental or vacation property.

The Exclusion Amount

You may be able to exclude from your taxable income, the gain from the sale of your main home, of up to $250,000 ($500,000 if filing MFJ). To qualify for this exclusion, all of the following must be true:

- You owned the home for at least 2 of the last 5 years (the ownership test).
- You lived in the home as your main home for at least 2 of the last 5 years (the use test).
- You did not exclude gain from the sale of another home during the 2-year period ending on the date of the sale.

If you are married, you can exclude up to $500,000 of the gain, but all of the following must be true:

- You filed a joint return with your spouse.
- Either you or your spouse meets the ownership test.
- Both you and your spouse meet the use test.
- Neither of you excluded gain from the sale of another home during the 2-year period ending on the date of the sale.

If one spouse dies, the surviving spouse may qualify to exclude up to $500,000 of any gain from the sale or exchange of his or her main home. To qualify for the exclusion, the surviving spouse must not remarry, must meet all the requirements for exclusion, and the sale must take place within two years after the date of the death of the spouse.

If you have more than one home, you can exclude gain only from the sale of your main home. You must pay tax on the gain realized from selling any other home. If you have two homes and live in both of them, your main home is ordinarily the one you live in most of the time.

You may be able to exclude gain from the sale of a home that you have used for business or to produce rental income, but you must meet the ownership and use tests. You can exclude any gain up to $250,000; however, you cannot exclude the part of the gain equal to the depreciation you claimed for renting the house.

The Selling Price

The selling price is the total amount you received for the home. If you received Form 1099-S from your broker, box 2 will show the gross proceeds you received for the house.
You must however, determine the net amount realized from the sale, which is the selling price of the house, minus all your selling expenses. Selling expenses include: advertising fees, commissions, legal fees, and loan charges paid by the seller.

The Adjusted Basis

If you made changes to your home, the adjusted basis (the original cost plus the amounts incurred on the improvements) will be used to figure the gain or loss.

Loss on Sale of Main Home

You cannot deduct a loss from the sale of your main home. A loss on the sale of your main home is a (nondeductible) personal loss. Also, the loss has no effect on the basis of a new residence purchased.

Home Abandoned, Foreclosed, or Repossessed

Generally, if a home is abandoned, foreclosed on, or repossessed, it is treated as a sale or a disposition, and any gain realized must be reported as taxable income. There are two possible consequences you must consider in these situations:

Taxable cancellation of debt income: Generally, a cancellation of debt is taxable income. When you borrowed the money, you were not required to include the loan proceeds in income, because you had an obligation to repay the lender. When that obligation is subsequently forgiven, the amount you received as loan proceeds is reportable as income, because you no longer have an obligation to repay the lender. However, in the case of non-recourse loans, a cancellation of debt is <u>not</u> taxable income. A non-recourse loan is a loan for which the lender's only remedy in case of default is to repossess the property being financed or used as collateral. That is, the lender cannot pursue you personally in case of default.

A reportable gain from the disposition of the home: As stated above, because foreclosures are treated like sales for tax purposes, any gains realized must be reported as taxable income.

When a house is foreclosed upon by the bank, you will typically receive a Form 1099-A from the lender, which will provide several pieces of relevant information. A foreclosure is treated as the sale of property, and you will need to calculate the gain or loss on the property. You will need the information on Form 1099-A, to report the foreclosure on your tax return.

To report the foreclosure, you will need to know the date of sale, and selling price of the property. Form 1099-A will provide you with the date of sale and the "selling price" of the property, but this is only half of the information that you will need to report the sale. The other half, which relates to the cost of the property, will be found in your escrow statements from when the property was purchased.

If the foreclosed property was your personal residence, you must report the foreclosure on Schedule D. You'll use the date of the foreclosure (box 1 of the 1099-A) as your date of sale, and you'll need to indicate the selling price. The selling price will be either the amount in box 2 or the amount in box 4. Which figure you'll use depends on the lending laws in the state where the property was located. You'll also need to indicate your purchase price or cost basis in the property. That information should be available from your closing statement from when you purchased the property. The difference between the selling price and your cost basis will result in your gain or loss. Gains are taxable income, whereas losses on personal residences are not tax-deductible. Any gain resulting on personal residences, however, can be offset by the capital gains exclusion for a main home.

If the foreclosed property was a rental property, you'll report the same information as above, but you'll use Form 4797, to report the recapture of any depreciation deductions you might have claimed on the property, and any passive activity loss carryovers. For rental properties, all gains are taxable and losses are deductible.

You might receive Form 1099-C instead of Form 1099-A, if the lender both foreclosed on the property and canceled any mortgage debt for which you was personally liable. If you receive a Form 1099-C, you must also report the foreclosure on Schedule D. The difference between the amount realized from the foreclosure (that is, the amount of the cancelled debt plus any other proceeds you may have received from the foreclosure), and your adjusted basis, is your gain or loss on the foreclosure or repossession. If there is a gain, it should be reported as a capital gain on Schedule D. However, as mentioned above, some or all of the gain from the sale of a personal residence qualifies for exclusion from income.

Like-Kind Exchanges

Whenever you sell business or investment property and you have a gain, you generally have to pay tax on the gain at the time of sale. Under Section 1031 of the IRC, however, if you reinvest the proceeds from the sale in similar property as part of a qualifying like-kind exchange, the tax code provides an exception, and allows you to postpone paying tax on the gain. It is very important to note that the gain from a like-kind exchange is not tax-free; it is only tax-deferred. You will eventually pay the tax on the gain if and when you dispose of the new property acquired in the exchange.

Note, however, that under the Tax Cuts and Jobs Act, Section 1031 now applies only to exchanges of real property and not to exchanges of personal or intangible property. An exchange of real property held primarily for sale still does not qualify as a like-kind exchange. Thus, effective January 1, 2018, exchanges of machinery, equipment, vehicles, artwork, collectibles, patents and other intellectual property and intangible business assets generally do not qualify for non-recognition of gain or loss as like-kind exchanges.

To qualify under the Section 1031 nontaxable exchange, a trade must meet the following conditions:

- The property must be business or investment property; it must not have been used for personal purposes.
- The property must not be held primarily for sale.
- The property to be received must be identified in writing within 45 days after the date you transferred the property given up in the exchange.
- The property to be received must be received by the earlier of: (a) the 180th day after the date on which you transferred the property given up in the trade, or (b) the due date, including extensions, for your tax return, for the year in which the transfer of the property given up occurs.

Reporting Other Gains or Losses

If you sell or dispose of property that you use in a trade or business, the sale must be reported on Form 4797, Sales of Business Property.

Form 4797 is used to record the following:

- The sale or trade of property used in a business.
- The involuntary conversion (from other than casualty or theft) of property used in a trade or business.
- Ordinary gains and losses on business property.
- The disposition of capital assets that are not reported on Schedule D.
- Gain from disposition of specific types of business property.
- The computation of recapture amounts under Sections 179, when the business use of Section 179 or listed property decreases to 50% or less.

Normally, a sale of business property does not result in a capital gain or loss, and is not subject to capital gains rules. However, if the property is subject to Section 1231 treatment, a capital gain or loss could result. Consequently, how the gains and losses from these transactions are treated (whether as ordinary or capital gain or loss) will depend on whether you have a net gain or a net loss from all section 1231 transactions.

If you have a net overall loss from section 1231 transactions, the loss is treated as an ordinary loss for tax purposes.

If you have a net overall section 1231 gain, the gain is considered ordinary income up to the amount of any section 1231 losses from the previous 5 years that have not been recaptured as ordinary income. The rest of the gain would be treated as a long-term capital gain.

14 Other Taxes

There are a number of other taxes you may owe, some of which include the following: (a) self-employment tax, (b) additional taxes on unreported tips, (c) additional taxes on the early withdrawal of retirement funds, (d) the first-time homebuyer credit repayment, and (e) household employment taxes. The objective of this chapter is to make you aware of all these taxes that you can potentially be liable for, and the possible penalties that can be imposed if you do not abide within the IRC rules.

The Alternative Minimum Tax (AMT)

Tax law provides tax benefits for taxpayers who earn certain types of income, and allows special deductions for taxpayers who incur certain kinds of expenses. The alternative minimum tax (AMT) attempts to ensure that anyone who benefits from these tax advantages pays at least a minimum amount of tax.

The AMT is a separately figured tax that eliminates many of the deductions and credits figured on the tax return, thus increasing the tax liability for an individual who would otherwise pay less tax. You may have to pay AMT if your taxable income for regular tax purposes, plus any adjustments and preference items that apply to you, exceed the AMT exemption amounts listed below.

The AMT exemption amounts for 2018 are as follows:

- $109,400 for MFJ or QW
- $70,300 for Single or HOH
- $54,700 for MFS

Under the new law the exemptions phase out at $1,000,000 for married individuals, and $500,000 for unmarried individuals.

You figure your AMT by completing Form 6251, Alternative Minimum Tax—Individuals.

- (Any off-the shelf tax software will effectively determine if you are liable for AMT, and will complete Form 6251 if required.)

Self-Employment Tax

If you have net earnings from self-employment of more than $400, you must file a tax return, and will be liable to pay self-employment tax. Self-employment tax is a tax consisting of Social Security and Medicare taxes, which is primarily imposed on individuals who work for themselves. It is similar to the Social Security and Medicare taxes withheld from the pay of most wage earners.

Unreported Social Security and Medicare Tax

If you work in an industry where it is customary to receive a portion of your income from customer tips, you are required to pay Social Security and Medicare taxes on those earnings. However, it is only possible to pay these taxes during the year if you report your tip income to your employer. If you receive cash and charge tips of $20 or more per month from any one job, you are required to report these to your employer. If you did not report all of these tips to your employer, you are required to report and pay the additional Social Security and Medicare taxes that should have been paid on these unreported tips. This you do as follows:

- You must complete Form 4137, Social Security and Medicare Tax on Unreported Tip Income. This form is used to calculate the tax in these unreported tips.
- You report the tax figured on Form 4137, on your tax return, and you must check box "a". You must attach Form 4137 to your tax return.

If you have allocated tips, these would have been shown separately in box 8 of your Form W-2, and would not be included in box 1 with your wages and reported tips. You must report your allocated tips as follows:

- Add the amount in box 8 of Form W-2 to the amount in box 1, and report the total as wages.
- You must complete Form 4137, and include the allocated tips on line 1.

Additional Taxes on Qualified Retirement Plans

To ensure that you are using your retirement funds for retirement purposes only, the government will penalized you if you take early withdrawals from the plan. Also, you can be penalized for excess accumulations in the plan. These penalties result in additional taxes.

Household Employment Taxes

You are considered to have a household employee if you hired someone to do household work, and that worker is your employee. The worker is considered your employee, if you can control not only what work is done, but also, how it is done. If the worker is your employee, it does not matter whether the work is full time or part time, or that you hired the worker through an agency or from a list provided by an agency or association. It also does not matter whether you pay the worker on an hourly, daily, or weekly basis, or by the job.

If you have a household employee, you may need to withhold and pay Social Security and Medicare taxes, and federal unemployment tax. You are not required to withhold federal income tax from your household employee's wages, but if your employee asks you to withhold it, you can.

You use Schedule H, Household Employment Taxes, to figure your total household employment taxes (Social Security, and Medicare). You add these household employment taxes to your income tax payable.

You should pay enough tax during the year to cover your household employment taxes, as well as your income tax. You may be subject to the estimated tax underpayment penalty, if you did not pay enough income and household employment taxes during the year.

You are required to complete Schedule H, Household Employment Taxes, if any of the following apply:

- You paid any one household employee cash wages of $1,700 or more in a calendar year.
- You withheld federal income tax at the request of any household employee.
- You paid cash wages of $1,000 or more in any one calendar quarter to all household employees.

You report household employment taxes on your tax return, and attach Schedule H to your tax return. You should not include amounts paid to an employee who was under 18 at any time during the year, and who was also a student.

First-Time Homebuyer Credit Repayment

If you claimed the first-time homebuyer credit for a home purchased in 2008, you are required to repay the credit over a period of 15 years. For homes purchased between April 8, 2008, and January 1, 2009, under the Housing and Economic Recovery Act, certain homeowners were eligible for a tax credit equal to 10 percent of the purchase price of a home, up to a maximum of $7,500 ($3,750 if MFS). This credit, in effect was not actually a credit, but was really an interest-free loan, which has to be repaid to the IRS over a 15-year period.

If your purchase occurred in 2008, you will have to repay one-fifteenth of this credit each year, as an additional tax. For example, an eligible taxpayer who claimed the maximum available credit of $7,500 on his or her 2008 federal income tax return must begin repaying the credit by including one-fifteenth of this amount ($500) as an additional tax, commencing on his or her 2010 tax return. Note, however, that the entire credit must be repaid in a single year, if the home ceases to be your main home. Generally, the amount of the repayment must first be entered on Form 5405, First-Time Homebuyer Credit and Repayment of the Credit.

15 Estimated Tax Payments, and Penalties

If you do not file your return and pay your tax by the due date, you may have to pay a penalty. You may also have to pay a penalty if you:

- Substantially understate your tax.
- Understate a reportable transaction.
- File an erroneous claim for a tax refund or credit.
- File a frivolous tax submission.

Also, if you provide fraudulent information on your tax return, you may have to pay a civil fraud penalty.

The objective of this chapter is to make you aware of your obligation as a taxpayer, to be as careful and as honest as you possibly can in your dealing with the IRS, and also of your obligation to pay at least 90% of your tax liability during the year, either through withholdings or through estimated payments. You will also be made aware of all the other potential penalties that you can avoid, simply by ensuring that you comply with all the relevant requirements of the tax code, as far as filing your returns and making the appropriate payments are concerned.

<u>Making Estimated Tax Payments</u>

Making estimated tax payments, is the method used to pay tax on income that is not subject to withholding. Income that is not subject to withholding includes income from self-employment, interest, dividends, alimony, rental, gains from the sale of assets, and prizes and awards won. You also may have to pay estimated tax if the amount of income tax being withheld from your salary, pension, or other income, is not enough to fully cover your expected tax liability for the current tax year.

If you're an employee, your employer will normally withhold taxes from your wages, and send these amounts to the IRS. Therefore, if all your income is from employment, you normally will not be required to make estimated tax payments.

If you do not pay enough through withholdings or estimated taxes, you may be charged a penalty. If you do not pay enough by the due date of each estimated tax payment period, you may also be charged a penalty, even if you are due a refund when you file your tax return.

Your estimated tax is the amount of tax liability you expect to have for a tax year, and you are expected to:

- Make a reasonable estimate of your tax liability before the tax year begins, or early in the tax year. You should use your prior year tax return as a guide for making this estimate.
- Pay most of this estimated tax as you earn the income during the year, either through withheld taxes, and/or by making estimated payments.

Tax law requires that you make estimated tax payments if the following conditions apply:

- You are an employee, but the amount of tax withheld from your salary or other income is not enough to cover the amount of tax you are required to pay, as you earn the related income during the year.
- You are self-employed, and expect to have net earnings.
- You receive interest, dividends, alimony, rent, or capital gains.

Are You Liable to Make Estimated Tax Payments?

You must determine at the beginning of the tax year, whether you need to make estimated tax payments during the year. To determine if you will be liable to pay estimated taxes, there are three basic tests you can apply. These are as follows:

- You do not need to make estimated tax payments if you expect to owe less than $1,000 in taxes for the tax year. This is computed by subtracting your federal income tax withholdings from the total amount of tax you expect to owe.
- You do not need to make estimated tax payments if you expect that your federal income tax withholdings, plus any estimated taxes paid, will amount to at least 90 percent of the tax that you expect to owe for this tax year.
- You're not required to make estimated tax payments if you expect that your income tax withholdings will be at least 100 percent of the tax on your previous year's tax return. (If your AGI was over $150,000 ($75,000 if filing MFS) the percentage is increased to 110 percent of the tax you owed for the previous year.)

If all your income is subject to withholding, you generally do not need to make estimated payments, as long as enough taxes were withheld. You start making estimated payments only in the period in which you expect to have income that will be subject to estimated tax.

Even if all your income is not subject to withholding, you do <u>not</u> have to make estimated payments if you had no tax liability for the prior year, or if you were not required to file a tax return for the prior year. However, your prior tax year must have covered a full 12-month period.

Generally, if you are married, you can choose to make joint or separate estimated tax payments. The choice to make either joint or separate estimated tax payments will not affect your right to file either MFJ or MFS.

How to Figure Your Estimated Tax Payments

The amount of estimated tax you are required to pay during the year, otherwise referred to as the required annual payment, is the **smaller** of: (a) 90% of the expected tax for the current tax year, or (b) 100% of the total tax on last year's tax return (110% of prior year tax, if income exceeds $150,000).

To figure both your estimated tax liability and your estimated payments, you should follow the five steps listed below:

1. The first step is to estimate your AGI for the year. In doing so, you must include all taxable income received, regardless of whether or not tax has been withheld for these incomes.
2. Subtract from your estimated AGI, the following: (a) your standard deduction or estimated itemized deductions, (b) your total exemptions, and (c) all credits you expect to claim.
3. To the above, add all other taxes you expect to owe.
4. You must complete the worksheet included with Form 1040-ES, Estimated Tax for Individuals, to figure your required annual payment, and keep it with your records.
5. You then subtract your expected withholdings from your required annual payment, and the difference will be the estimated payment you are required to make.

If you expect your annual estimated income to remain constant throughout the year, you use the regular installment method to figure your quarterly payments, simply by dividing the payment you expect to make for the year by 4.

If you do not earn your income evenly throughout the year, you can use the annualized installment method to figure your quarterly payments.

When to Make Estimated Payments

You must pay enough by the due date of each payment period, to avoid a penalty for that period. Tax law divides the year into four estimated tax payment periods. The due dates for making estimated payments are: April 15, June 15, September 15, and January 15 of the following year. Note however that:

- You do not have to make the January 15 payment if you file your tax return and pay the rest of the tax you owe by January 31.
- You do not have to make estimated tax payments until you have earned enough income on which you will owe tax.
- If during the year, there have been changes in your income, exemptions, etc., then you must refigure your estimate tax, and pay the new amount by the next due date, or in installments.

How to Make Estimated Payments

You make your quarterly payments by sending them in to the IRS with the payment vouchers that are attached to Form 1040-ES. You can make all or part of your payment by credit card or check. If you're paying by check, be sure to record your Social Security number, and the tax year for which you are making payment, in the memo area of the check.

As a means of making estimated payments, you can also opt to credit a refund on your current year's tax return, to next year's estimated tax payments. You do this by entering the amount you want credited to next year's estimated payments, on your current Form 1040. This amount, you can elect to be credited in full to your first quarterly payment, or you can spread it out among any or all of your quarterly payments. Once you credit your refund to your estimated tax, you cannot have it refunded to you after the first due date of April 15.

IRS Penalties

Taxpayers in the United States may face various penalties for failures related to their federal, state, or local tax matters. Most Penalties are of a monetary nature, but some may involve forfeiture of property, or might even include jail time. Most monetary penalties are based on the amount of tax that was not properly paid. Penalties usually increase with the period of nonpayment. Some penalties are fixed dollar amounts, or fixed percentages of some measure required to be reported. Some penalties may be waived or abated where the taxpayer can prove reasonable cause for the failure.

Underpayment Penalties

If you did not pay enough tax throughout the year, either through withholding, or by making estimated tax payments, you may have to pay a penalty for underpayment of estimated tax. Generally, most taxpayers will avoid this penalty if they owe less than $1,000 in tax, after subtracting their withholdings and credits, **or** if they paid at least 90% of the tax for the current year, or 100% of the tax shown on the return for the prior year, whichever is smaller.

If you are an employee, and you did not have enough tax withheld from your wages, or if you are self-employed, you will be required to make quarterly payments of estimated tax. The minimum payment for each payment period is usually one quarter of your required annual payment. If you do not make the required payments, you will be subject to the underpayment penalty.

The rules concerning the underpayment penalty are as follows:

- Generally, you will owe a penalty if your total payment (estimated taxes and withholdings) is less than your required annual payment.
- Because the penalty for quarterly taxes is figured separately for each payment period, you may owe a penalty for an underpayment in a particular period, even if you made up for the underpayment in a later payment period.
- If you do not pay enough tax by each quarterly due date, you may owe a penalty even if you are due a refund when you file your tax return.

Generally, you will not be liable for an underpayment penalty, if either of the following conditions apply to you:

- Your total tax minus your withholdings and refundable credits, is less than $1,000.
- Your total tax was zero for the prior tax year, or you were not required to file a tax return for that year. You must, however, have been a US citizen or resident for the entire year, and your tax year was at least a 12-month period.

In most cases, you do not need to figure your penalty yourself; the IRS will do it for you and send you a bill. If you want the IRS to figure the penalty, you must leave the estimated penalty line blank. You will not owe interest on the penalty as long as you pay it by the due date specified by the IRS bill.
If you wish to figure the penalty yourself, you must do so by completing Form 2210, Underpayment of Estimated Tax by Individuals, Estates, and Trusts.

You must, however, figure the penalty yourself if any of the following conditions apply:

- If you request a waiver of the penalty.
- If you use the annualized income installment method.
- If you use your actual withholdings as your estimated tax payments, and treat them as paid on the dates withheld, instead of in equal amounts on the payment due dates.
- If you based your required installments on your prior year tax and you filed, or are filing MFJ in either prior or current year, but not for both years.

You can use the less complicated short method (Part III of Form 2210) to figure your penalty as a percentage of your total underpayment if you: (a) made no estimated tax payments during the year, or (b) paid your estimated taxes in four equal payments.

You can receive a waiver of the penalty for underpayment, if the IRS can determine that:

- You were not able to make a payment because you suffered a casualty, disaster, or other unusual circumstance, and that it would be inequitable to impose the penalty.
- You retired (after reaching age 62) or became disabled during the tax year when a payment was due, or during the preceding year, and the underpayment was due to reasonable cause, and not willful neglect.

It is very important to understand that you can incur interest and further penalties in addition to the underpayment penalty. To avoid these additional interest and penalties, it is best to pay the full amount you owe when you file your return.

Failure-to-File Penalty

If you do not file your tax return by the deadline (including extensions) you might face a failure-to-file penalty. The failure-to-file penalty begins calculating the day after the due date for filing the tax return. The typical due date for filling a tax return is April 15th, if an extension has not been applied for. If an extension has been filed for and accepted before the April 15th due date, then the adjusted due date is October 15th.

The failure-to-file rules are as follows:

- The penalty for filing late is usually 5 percent of the unpaid taxes for each month or part of a month that a return is late.

181

- The penalty is limited to a maximum of 25% of the balance due.
- If you file your return more than 60 days after the due date or extended due date, the minimum penalty is the smaller of $135 or 100 percent of the unpaid tax.
- The penalty may not be charged if you can show that you failed to file on time because of reasonable cause, and not because of willful neglect.

If both the failure-to-file penalty and the failure-to-pay penalty (see below) apply in any month, the 5 percent failure-to-file penalty is reduced by the failure-to-pay penalty.

The failure-to-file penalty is considerably more than the failure-to-pay penalty. So if you cannot pay all the taxes you owe, you should still file your tax return on time, and explore other payment options in the meantime. The IRS will work with you.

Failure-to-Pay Penalty

If you do not pay your taxes by the due date, you will generally have to pay a failure-to-pay penalty. The failure-to-pay penalty is calculated based on the amount of tax you owe. The penalty is calculated from the original payment deadline (the April 15th filing deadline) until the balance due is paid in full.

The failure-to-pay rules are as follows:

- The failure-to-pay penalty is usually ½ of 1% of any tax (other than estimated tax) not paid by the regular due date.
- This penalty can be as much as 25% of your unpaid taxes.
- If you timely filed a request for an extension of time to file, and you paid at least 90 percent of your actual tax liability by the original due date, you will not be faced with a failure-to-pay penalty, as long as the remaining balance is paid by the extended due date.
- The penalty may not be charged if you can show that you failed to pay on time because of reasonable cause, and not because of willful neglect.

Accuracy Related Penalties

If you are audited, and the IRS discovers that you have: (a) understated income, (b) took improper tax deductions or credits, or (c) prepared an inaccurate tax return, you will be sent a tax bill. This tax bill normally contains tax penalties and interest. If these mistakes were not deliberate or fraudulent; but occurred because of carelessness on your part, you will be served with an accuracy related penalty.

An accuracy-related penalty of 20% is applied to any underpayment of tax that is due to: (a) substantial understatement of income tax, (b) negligence, or (c) intentional disregard of rules or regulations.

Substantial understatement

If you understate your tax liability, the penalty depends on whether the understatement is substantial or not. Income tax is substantially understated if the understatement of the tax liability exceeds the greater of: (a) 10% of the correct tax, or (b) $5,000.

You may be able to avoid the substantial understatement penalty if you can prove that you have a reasonable basis for your position, accompanied by good faith.

Negligence

Negligence can be defined as the failure or lack of any reasonable effort to comply with IRS rules and regulations, and not using proper care in preparing a tax return. Some examples of negligence include the following:

- A failure to keep proper records to support credits or deductions claimed.
- A failure to reasonably check the accuracy of a deduction you claimed, which you were not eligible for.
- A failure to include income on your tax return that was clearly shown in an information form (like a 1099), as income you earned.

You may not have to pay a negligence penalty if you can prove that there was a reasonable cause for the error.

Intentional disregard of rules and regulations

Intentional disregard includes the careless, reckless, or intentional disregard of the tax code when you prepared your tax return. Your actions would be considered careless if you did not illustrate reasonable diligence to determine whether an item on your return was correct.

Penalty for Fraudulent Tax Returns

If the IRS serves you with an audit that clearly shows that in order to pay less tax, you intentionally and fraudulently under-reported or omitted income, you could be faced with a penalty of 75 percent of the underpayment that is due to the fraudulent position. Besides the financial penalties, you could also be charged with tax evasion or have other criminal charges brought against you. Note that a taxpayer, who files a tax return subjectively believing that it is correct, is not regarded as having filed a "fraudulent" return, even if the return contains errors, as long as he or she sincerely believes the return complies with the law. To prove the return fraudulent, the government will normally rely on such factors as a taxpayer's education, experience, and knowledge of financial affairs.

Fraud can constitute any of the following:

- The purposeful avoidance of record keeping.
- Underreporting or omitting income or assets.
- Destroying or altering evidence, such as accounting books, logs, receipts or other records.
- Lying to IRS agents during an audit investigation.
- Keeping two separate sets of books.
- Claiming nonexistent dependents.

Again, note that negligence or ignorance of the law does not constitute fraud.

Penalty for Filing Frivolous Returns

A frivolous tax return is one that does not include enough information to figure the correct tax, or one that contains information clearly showing that the tax you reported is substantially incorrect. Also, a frivolous act includes a desire to delay or interfere with the administration of federal income tax laws, or where an individual files their taxes based on unsubstantiated legal arguments.

If you file a frivolous tax return, the IRS can impose a penalty of $5,000 on you (and a similar penalty on your spouse, if you file a joint return).

If you receive a letter from the IRS that says you have been charged a frivolous return tax penalty, you need to contact them immediately. You will have to pay the fine, and then you can appeal the ruling if you have just cause.

Penalty for Bounced Checks

If the check you use to pay the IRS bounces, they can charge you a penalty. The penalty is 2 percent of the amount of the check - unless the check is under $1,250, in which case the penalty is the amount of the check, or $25, whichever is less.

16 Filing for Extensions, Amended Returns, Installment Agreements, and Offers in Compromise

The objective of this chapter is to make you aware of some rights that you have as a taxpayer: These rights include the following: (a) your right to file for an extension if you believe that you will not be able to make the April 15 deadline, (b) your right to file an amended tax return, to correct a previously filed one, and (c) your right to negotiate an installment agreement or an offer in compromise, if you cannot pay your taxes in full.

How to File for an Extension

If you believe that you will not be able to file your tax return by the due date (generally April 15) you can apply for an automatic six-month extension of time to file, by filing Form 4868, Application for Automatic Extension of Time to File U.S. Individual Income Tax Return. With the 6-month extension, you must file your tax return by October 15.

It is very important to note that when you file for an extension, you are only requesting an extension of time to file, and **not** an extension of time to pay. Therefore, you have an obligation to make an accurate estimate of your tax liability for the year, and pay the amount due by regular due date (April 15). If you do not pay the taxes due, you could be hit with a penalty.

When you file for an extension, you should enter any payment you enclose with Form 4868. If you cannot pay the full amount of the tax you owe, you can still get the extension, but you may owe interest on the unpaid amount, and possibly a penalty for paying late.

If you are outside of the U.S. you are allowed an automatic two-month extension to file and pay federal income tax due if:

- You are a US citizen or resident, and on the regular due date of the tax return, you are living outside the US and Puerto Rico, and your main place of business or post of duty is outside the US and Puerto Rico.
- You are a US citizen or resident, and you are in military or naval service, on active duty outside the US and Puerto Rico.

How to File an Amended Return

If subsequent to filing your tax return, you discover that errors were made, you should file an amended tax return to correct these errors. Naturally, this corrective information will alter your tax calculations. The following are some of the typical errors you can make on your tax return:

- You did not report all of your income. For example, you received a W-2 with additional income, which arrived after you filed your original return.
- You claimed deductions or credits on your original tax return that you were not eligible for, and need to remove them.
- Conversely, you subsequently discovered that you did not claim all the deductions or credits you should have claimed, and need to include them.
- You need to make a correction to your filing status.

You should not file an amended return if you are only correcting mathematical errors, as the IRS computers will check your math and correct any errors in the calculation. Mathematical errors are errors made in adding or subtracting items on your tax return.

To file an amended return, you must use Form 1040X, Amended U.S. Individual Income Tax Return.

The following rules relate to filing amended returns:

- Form 1040X cannot be filed electronically, and must be mailed in as a paper return.
- You must file a separate Form 1040X for each year being amended.
- An amended return will usually result in either additional tax due, or a refund owed to you. If you are due a refund, interest might be paid on it.
- You must file Form 1040X within three years after the date you filed the original return, or within two years after the date you paid the tax, whichever is later.
- If you did not file an original return when due, generally you can claim a refund by filing a return within three years from the date the tax was paid.

Note that if you file an amended federal return, you should also amend your state tax return.

How to Negotiate an Installment Agreement

If you have a balance due, and you cannot pay all or part of it when you file your tax return, you can request an installment agreement from the IRS. An installment agreement is an agreement you make with the IRS, which will allow you to pay off the liability by making monthly payments. You must still file your tax return on time, even if you cannot pay, otherwise, you will be hit with a penalty. During the course of an installment agreement, penalties and interest continue to accrue. Generally, no levies may be served during installment agreements.

How to Apply for an Installment Agreement

To request an installment agreement, you must complete Form 9465, Installment Agreement Request, and file it with your tax return. In completing Form 9465, you must enter the following information: (a) the amount you owe, (b) the amount of the payment you are making with the tax return, and (c) the amount you propose to pay each month.

To apply for an installment agreement, you must observe the following rules:

- You can apply online if you owe $25,000 or less, in combined individual income tax, penalties and interest.
- You must complete and mail in Form 9465.
- If you owe more than $25,000, you will also need to complete Form 433-F, Collection Information Statement.

You will generally receive a response from the IRS within 30 days, if you file before March 31. If your request is approved, the IRS will charge you a set up fee. In addition to the fee, you will be charged interest on the balance due, until it is paid in full.

Your request for an installment agreement cannot be turned down if you owe $10,000 or less in taxes, and ALL three of the following situations apply:

- During the last five years, you have filed all income tax returns on time, and paid any income tax due, and have not entered into a previous installment agreement for the payment of tax.
- The IRS determines that you cannot pay the tax owed in full when it is due. You must, however, be able to provide the IRS with any information needed to make that determination.
- You agree to pay the full amount you owe within three years, and to comply with the tax laws while the agreement is in effect.

To keep your account in good standing with the IRS, you must ensure that you do the following:

- Pay at least your minimum monthly payment when it's due. (Direct debit or payroll deductions make this easy.)
- Include your name, address, SSN, daytime phone number, tax year, and return type on your payment.
- File all required tax returns on time.
- Pay all taxes you owe in full, and on time. You should contact the IRS to change your existing agreement if you cannot meet your obligations.
- Continue to make all scheduled payments, even if the IRS should apply a refund due to you, against your account balance.

How to Apply for an Offer in Compromise

If you are unable to settle your tax debt in full, you can apply the IRS for an Offer in Compromise. An offer in compromise allows you to settle your tax debt for less than the full amount you owe. It's an option available if you can't pay your full tax liability, or if doing so would create a financial hardship for you.

The IRS upon receipt of such an application will consider your unique set of facts and circumstances, which will include:

- Your ability to pay.
- Your income.
- Your expenses.
- Your asset equity.

The IRS generally approves an offer in compromise when the amount offered represents the most they can expect to collect from that taxpayer within a reasonable period of time.

Submitting the Offer

You'll find step-by-step instructions and all the forms for submitting an offer, in the Offer in Compromise Booklet, Form 656-B. You can also view the "Complete Form 656" video on the IRS website.

In general, your completed offer package should include the following:

- A completed Form 433-A, Collection Information Statement for Wage Earners and Self-Employed Individuals, and all other required documentation as specified on the forms
- A completed Form 656, Offer in Compromise.

- A non-refundable application fee.
- A non-refundable initial payment.

In applying for an OIC, you must select a payment option. Your initial payment will vary based on your offer and the payment option you choose. You can choose either of the following two payment options:

- **Lump Sum Cash:** You should submit an initial payment of 20 percent of the total offer amount with your application. Wait for written acceptance, and if accepted, you then pay the remaining balance of the offer in five or fewer payments.
- **Periodic Payment:** You should submit your initial payment with your application. Continue to pay the remaining balance in monthly installments while the IRS considers your offer. If accepted, continue to pay monthly until it is paid in full.

You should note however, that if you meet the Low Income Certification guidelines, you do **not** have to send the application fee or the initial payment, and you will **not** need to make monthly installments during the evaluation of your offer. You must check your application package for the details, to see whether you qualify for the Low Income Certification.

It's entirely up to the IRS to accept or reject your offer in compromise, but while your offer is being evaluated, the following process takes place:

- Your non-refundable payments and fees will be applied to the tax liability (you may designate payments to a specific tax year and tax debt).
- A Notice of Federal Tax Lien may be filed.
- Other collection activities are suspended.
- The legal assessment and collection period is extended.
- You should make all required payments associated with your offer.
- You are not required to make payments on an existing installment agreement.
- You can consider your offer as being automatically accepted if the IRS does not make a determination within two years of the IRS receipt date.

17 Injured Spouse Situations

Many married taxpayers choose to file a joint tax return because of the benefits to be derived from this filing status. On a joint return, both taxpayers are jointly and individually responsible for the tax and any interest or penalty due on the return, even if they later divorce. This is true even if a divorce decree should state that your former spouse will be solely responsible for any amounts due on previously filed joint returns.

The situation can exist, then, where one spouse could be held responsible for all the tax due, even if all the income was earned by the other spouse. In cases like this, the IRS, in the interest of equity may allow a spouse in such a situation to be relieved of tax, interest, and penalties that are due on the joint tax return.

Before we go any further, however, we must make a very important distinction between an injured spouse and an innocent spouse.

Injured spouse
If you're married and your spouse has an unpaid tax liability on a joint return that you filed together, it is likely that the IRS will withhold the total refund, including the part that's due to you, to offset some or all of your spouse's liability. In this case, you can be considered an injured spouse.

Innocent spouse
The situation also exists when one spouse who knows nothing about the filing of the tax return, finds himself or herself responsible for the tax liability of the other spouse. In this case, he or she may be considered an innocent spouse.

The Injured Spouse Allocation

Generally, if a taxpayer owes past-due federal tax, state income tax, child or spousal support, or certain federal non-tax debts such as student loans, etc., all or part of any refund due to the taxpayer may be used to pay (offset) the past due amount. If you filed a joint tax return with your spouse, who owes a federal or state obligation, all or part of your tax refund will usually be applied to your spouse's past due debt. Tax law, however, allows you to claim a relief under the injured spouse allocation, to ensure that the IRS does not withhold your part of the tax refund. Therefore, if only one spouse owes the liability, under this provision, the other spouse may be entitled to claim his or her share of the refund.

If the tax refund on your joint return has been withheld by the IRS, because your spouse has a past-due debt, you can get back your share of the tax refund by filing Form 8379, Injured Spouse Allocation. You can file Form 8379 with Form 1040, or you can file it as a stand-alone form after Form 1040 has been filed.

If you consider yourself an injured spouse, you will be eligible to file Form 8379, only if all the following conditions apply:

- You must not be the party who is required to pay the past-due amount.
- You must have reported some sort of income such as wages, taxable interest, etc., on the joint return.
- You must have made or reported payments such as federal tax withheld from your wages or estimated tax payments, or must have claimed a refundable credit, such as the earned income credit or the additional child tax credit.

If your home was in a community property state during the year, you may file Form 8379 even if only one condition above applies.

On Form 8379, you must allocate the following between you and your spouse:

- Adjustments.
- Exemptions.
- Credits.
- Other taxes.
- Payments shown on the tax return.

Based on the allocations you made on Form 8379, the IRS will figure the amount of any refund due to the injured spouse. The injured spouse allocation is used only to get a refund of **your** part of a tax refund that would otherwise have been used to pay your spouse's past-due debt.

The Innocent Spouse Relief

By requesting the innocent spouse relief, you can be relieved of the responsibility for paying tax, interest, and penalties, if your spouse (or former spouse) improperly reported items, or omitted items on your joint tax return. To request the innocent spouse relief, you need to file Form 8857, Request for Innocent Spouse Relief, with the IRS.

An innocent spouse can get relief when the other spouse makes false reports on a joint tax return. The IRS offers innocent parties a way to get out from under tax debt liability that is the result of mistakes or errors made by the other party on a joint tax return. The IRS created the innocent spouse relief because situations do arise where it would be unfair to hold a spouse liable for the tax liability that was created by the other spouse.

It is very important that the innocent spouse relief should not be confused with the injured spouse allocation defined above. By requesting innocent spouse relief, you can be relieved of the responsibility for paying tax, interest, and penalties if your spouse (or former spouse) improperly reported or omitted items on your joint tax return. If the relief is granted, the tax, interest, and penalties that qualify for the relief, will be collected <u>only</u> from your spouse (or former spouse).

However, you are jointly and individually responsible for any tax, interest, and penalties that do not qualify for the relief; and the IRS will collect these amounts from either you or your spouse (or former spouse).

After you file Form 8857, it is the IRS, which will figure the amount of the liability (if any) that you are responsible for; you are not required to figure this amount yourself.

You must meet all of the following conditions, to qualify for the innocent spouse relief:

- You filed a joint return, which has an understatement of tax, due to erroneous items (defined below) of your spouse (or former spouse).
- You can establish that at the time you signed the joint return, you did not know, and had no reason to know, that there was an understatement of tax.
- You are able to prove that the understatement of tax did not bring a significant benefit to you. The deception would not be considered a significant benefit simply because your spouse supports you.
- Taking into account all the facts and circumstances, it would be unfair to hold you liable for the understatement.
- You and your spouse (or former spouse), did not transfer property to one another as part of a fraudulent scheme. A fraudulent scheme includes a scheme to defraud the IRS or other third party, such as a creditor, ex-spouse, or business partner.

Erroneous items can fall into either of the following category:

- Unreported income. This is any gross income received by your spouse (or former spouse) that is not reported.

- Incorrect deduction, credit, or basis. This is any improper deduction, credit, or property basis claimed by your spouse (or former spouse).

18 Reporting Foreign Financial Assets

The United States taxes its citizens and resident aliens on their worldwide income, and allows any income tax which they must pay to foreign jurisdictions, as a credit against their U.S. tax liability.

FBAR Reporting

U.S. law requires that a person with a financial interest in, or signature authority over, foreign financial accounts, must file Form TD F 90-22.1, Report of Foreign Financial Accounts (FBAR), if the total value of such accounts exceeds $10,000 at any time during the calendar year. The FBAR is due to be filed by the following June 30.

A person, who is required to file an FBAR, but who fails to timely and properly file the FBAR, is subject to a civil penalty of $10,000 for each violation. If there is reasonable cause for the violation, and the account balance is reported, no penalty will be imposed. A person, who <u>willfully</u> fails to report a foreign financial account, or fails to report account identifying information, is subject to a civil penalty equal to the **greater** of $100,000, or 50% of the account balance at the time of the violation. Willful violation is also subject to criminal prosecution.

Form 8938 Reporting

The Hiring Incentives to Restore Employment Act, Section 511, enacted March 18, 2010, imposes a <u>new</u> reporting requirement for foreign financial assets, in addition to the requirement of filing an FBAR. Codified as Internal Revenue Code Section 6038D, the new law applies to specified persons with specified foreign financial assets which satisfy the reporting threshold.

The new law requires Form 8938, Statement of Specified Foreign Assets, to be filed with the specified person's U.S. income tax return.

A specified person is an individual who is:

- A U.S. citizen;
- A resident alien of the U.S.;
- A nonresident alien who makes an election to be treated as a resident alien for purposes of filing a joint income tax return; or

- A nonresident alien who is a bona fide resident of American Samoa or Puerto Rico.

"Specified person" will include a domestic entity once the IRS issues regulations covering same.

Specified foreign financial assets include:

- Any financial account maintained by a foreign financial institution; and
- To the extent held for investment, and not in a financial account: (a) any stock or securities issued by someone that is not a U.S. person, (b) any interest in a foreign entity, and (c) any financial instrument or contract with an issuer or counterparty that is not a U.S. person.

Note that a partnership interest is not held for investment, if the holder uses it in the conduct of a trade or business. Stock is not considered used or held in the conduct of a trade or business.

"Foreign financial assets" reportable on Form 8938 is thus broader than "foreign financial account" reportable on an FBAR.

The Reporting Threshold

An individual who is not married, or who is married and files separately for U.S. income tax purposes, and who <u>does not</u> live abroad, must file Form 8938 if the total value of his or her foreign financial assets exceeds (a) $50,000 on the last day of the tax year, or (b) $75,000 on any day during the tax year. A married couple who file a joint income tax return (and hence file a joint Form 8938) must file Form 8938 if the total value of their foreign financial assets exceeds (a) $100,000 on the last day of the tax year, or (b) $150,000 on any day during the tax year.

An individual who is not married, or who is married, but files as married filing separately, and who <u>does</u> live abroad, must file Form 8938 if the total value of his or her foreign financial assets exceeds (a) $200,000 on the last day of the tax year, or (b) $300,000 on any day during the year. A married couple who live abroad and file a joint income tax return must file Form 8938 if the total value of their foreign financial assets exceeds (a) $400,000 on the last day of the tax year, or (b) $600,000 on any day during the year.

If the above thresholds are not met, then taxpayers are not required to file Form 8938.

An individual lives abroad for this purpose if he or she is:

- A U.S. citizen who has been a bona fide resident of a foreign country or countries for an uninterrupted period that includes the entire tax year; or
- A U.S. citizen or resident who is present in a foreign country or countries at least 330 full days during any period of 12 consecutive months that ends in the tax year being reported.

A married couple who file a joint income tax return, and thus file a joint Form 8938, should report joint foreign financial assets only once on their Form 8938.

For a married couple filing separate income tax returns, each spouse is deemed to own one-half of jointly-owned foreign financial assets for threshold reporting purposes.

Where a specified individual owns a foreign financial asset jointly with someone who is not his or her spouse; or with a spouse who is not a specified individual, each joint owner is deemed to own all of the specified foreign financial asset.

The new Form 8938 filing requirement does not replace or otherwise affect a taxpayer's obligation to file Form TD F 90-22.1. Individuals must file each form for which they meet the relevant reporting threshold.

Reportable assets do not include the following:

- Financial account held at a U.S. branch of a foreign financial institution.
- Domestic mutual fund investing in foreign stocks and securities.
- Foreign real estate held directly.
- Foreign currency held directly.
- Precious Metals held directly.
- Personal property, held directly, such as art, antiques, jewelry, cars and other collectibles.
- 'Social Security'- type program benefits provided by a foreign government.

19 The Affordable Care Act (ACA)

Beginning in tax year 2014, under the Affordable Care Act, the Federal government, State governments, insurers, employers, and individuals share the responsibility for health insurance coverage. If you already have qualifying health insurance coverage (called minimum essential coverage), you do not need to do anything more than maintaining that coverage. Previously, if you did not have coverage, and were not eligible for an exemption, you would have to purchase coverage through the Health Insurance Marketplace, or risk having to pay a penalty. The new law, however, now longer requires you to make a shared responsibility payment (penalty), if you fail to purchase health insurance. In other words, the penalty has been abolished.

The Health Insurance Marketplace is actually an online health insurance exchange, giving individuals and small businesses the opportunity to evaluate health insurance and make an informed decision about what to buy. The Health Insurance Marketplace is effectively your one-stop shop to find your new health care plan. The Marketplace is an online shopping site where individuals and small businesses can compare and buy health insurance. If your employer doesn't offer insurance, and you are not eligible to claim an exemption; to avoid a penalty, you will have to use the Marketplace to browse plans and select your insurance. If you purchase your insurance coverage through the Health Insurance Marketplace, you may be eligible for a Premium Tax Credit (PTC).

Also, to facilitate these changes to the tax laws, 5 new forms have been created. These forms are listed below:

- Form 8965 – Health Coverage Exemptions.
- Form 8962 – Premium Tax Credit (PTC).
- Form 1095-A – Health Insurance Marketplace Statement.
- Form 1095-B – Health Coverage.
- Form 1095-C – Employer-Provided Health Insurance Offer and Coverage.

Premium Tax Credit

If you purchase health insurance coverage through the Marketplace, you may be eligible for the Premium Tax Credit (PTC), which is available to people with moderate incomes. Note that only taxpayers who purchased a qualified health plan from a State-based or Federally-facilitated Health Insurance

Marketplace (Marketplace) may be eligible for the Premium Tax Credit. This is a new federal tax credit to help eligible taxpayers pay for health insurance premiums.

When enrolling in a qualified health plan through the Marketplace, eligible taxpayers can choose to have some or all of the benefit of the credit paid in advance to their insurance company as advance credit payments, or wait to claim all of the benefit of the premium tax credit on their tax return. Taxpayers must file a tax return to claim the premium tax credit.

Any advance payments (subsidy) made to the insurance company during the year are subtracted from the Premium Tax Credit calculated on the tax return.

Those who choose advance credit payments must file a tax return to reconcile their advance credit payments with their actual Premium Tax Credit, even if they have gross income that is below the income tax filing threshold.

Depending on your circumstances, you may be entitled to more credit, or may have to pay a portion of the subsidy back, and this would impact any tax refund or balance due.

Whether you receive a subsidy during the year or not, you must file Form 8962 with your federal income tax return in order to reconcile the subsidy and credit.

Premium Tax Credit Eligibility
The Premium Tax Credit is a refundable tax credit that helps eligible people with moderate incomes afford health insurance purchased through the Health Insurance Marketplace.

If you are eligible for the credit, you can choose to:

- Get it now: Have some or all of the estimated credit paid in advance on your behalf directly to your insurance company, to lower what you pay out-of-pocket for your monthly premiums during the current year These payments are called advance payments of the premium tax credit.

OR

- Get it later: Wait to get the credit when you file your tax return in the following year. This means, then, that no advance payments would be made to your insurance provider during the year.

Advance credit payments made to your insurance company are based on an estimate of the credit that you will claim on your federal income tax return. The Marketplace estimates the credit by using information about your family composition and projected income that you provide when you submit your application.

To be eligible for the Premium Tax Credit, all of the following must apply:

- Your income must be between 100% and 400% of Federal Poverty Line (see below) for a given family size.

- You cannot be claimed as a dependent.

- If married, you must file a joint return (although some exceptions may apply).

- You must be enrolled in a qualified health plan through Marketplace.

- Cannot be eligible for other minimum essential coverage.

- Premiums must be paid.

The Federal Poverty Line (FPL)

The federal poverty line (FPL) is an income amount determined by the U.S. Department of Health and Human Services (HHS), which is adjusted for family size and considered the poverty level for the year. The HHS determines the federal poverty line amounts annually and publishes a table reflecting these amounts at the beginning of each calendar year.

The HHS provides three federal poverty lines:

- One for residents of the 48 contiguous states and D.C.,
- One for Alaska residents, and
- One for Hawaii residents.

The federal poverty line (FPL) is the indicator used to determine if you are eligible for the Premium Tax Credit; and if you are eligible, how much of the credit you will be eligible for.

The size of the Premium Tax Credit is calculated on a sliding scale basis. Therefore, a taxpayer with household income at 200 percent of the FPL for the taxpayer's family size will get a larger credit to help cover the cost of insurance, than a taxpayer with the same family size who has household income at 300 percent of the FPL. In other words, the higher the household income, the lower the amount of the credit.

If you receive advance payment of the Premium Tax Credit to help pay for your insurance premiums, you should report all changes, such as income or family size, to your Marketplace when they happen.

It is important for you to report changes in circumstances, in order to get the proper type and amount of financial assistance, and to avoid getting too much or too little in advance. Reporting changes in circumstances will allow the Marketplace to adjust your advance credit payments.

In other words, reporting changes will make sure you get the correct amount of the advance payment of the credit. Receiving too much or too little in advance can affect your refund or balance due when you file your tax return. This will help you avoid getting a smaller refund or owing money that you did not expect to owe on your federal tax return.

Changes you should report to the Marketplace include the following:

- Birth or adoption.
- Marriage or divorce.
- Change of address during year.
- Changes in household income.
- Incarceration or release from incarceration.
- Gaining or losing health care coverage or eligibility.
- Other changes affecting income or household size.

Whether you choose to get the credit now by receiving advance credit payments, or later, by claiming the premium tax credit, you must file a federal income tax return.

If you choose to have the credit paid in advance, you will have to reconcile the advance payments with the actual credit you compute when you file your tax return. When you file your tax return, you will subtract the total of any advance payments you received during the year from the amount of the Premium Tax Credit calculated on your tax return. This is done by completing Form 8962 (see below). On this form, you compare the advance payments with the amount of credit for which you are eligible.

If the advance payments are more than the credit for which you are eligible, this means that the advance payments would have been overpaid, and that you will have to repay the excess advance payments, subject to a repayment cap (see below). This will invariable affect your tax refund or balance due. If you are entitled to more credit than you have already received via advance payments, the additional credit will be claimed on your tax return, and this will either increase your refund or lower your balance due.